Home

Homeless

Narratives from the Streets

JOSHUA D. PHILLIPS

McFarland & Company, Inc., Publishers
Jefferson, North Carolina

LIBRARY OF CONGRESS CATALOGUING-IN-PUBLICATION DATA

Names: Phillips, Joshua Daniel, author.
Title: Homeless : narratives from the streets / Joshua D. Phillips.
Description: Jefferson, North Carolina : McFarland & Company, Inc.,
    Publishers, 2016. | Includes bibliographical references and index.
Identifiers: LCCN 2016036008 | ISBN 9781476664576 (softcover :
    acid free paper)
Subjects: LCSH: Homelessness—United States. | Homeless persons—
    United States. | United States—Social policy.
Classification: LCC HV4505 .P485 2016 | DDC 362.5/920973—dc23
LC record available at https://lccn.loc.gov/2016036008

BRITISH LIBRARY CATALOGUING DATA ARE AVAILABLE

ISBN (print) 978-1-4766-6457-6
ISBN (ebook) 978-1-4766-2527-0

Front cover images © 2016 iStock

Printed in the United States of America

*McFarland & Company, Inc., Publishers
    Box 611, Jefferson, North Carolina 28640
        www.mcfarlandpub.com*

For my brother Siddiq

Acknowledgments

There are numerous people to whom I owe a great amount of gratitude. First, I would like to acknowledge the staff and clientele of Good Samaritan Ministries in Carbondale, Illinois, for allowing me access to their facilities, their work, and their stories. Without their openness and cooperation, this book would not exist. Next, I would like to thank several faculty members at Southern Illinois University who helped with this research. Foremost, I cannot express enough gratitude to Dr. Suzanne Daughton. Without her guidance and compassion, I would have been lost in this process. I cannot thank her enough for her time, energy, and efforts. Furthermore, Dr. Nathan Stucky deserves a great deal of recognition as the idea for this project first originated and took shape in his classroom. Additionally, I would like to thank Dr. Satoshi Toyosaki, Dr. Sandy Pensoneau-Conway, Dr. Ann Fischer, and Dr. Rebecca Walker for their roles in this project.

I would also like to acknowledge my dear friends who took the time to read, edit, and offer feedback on the final version of this manuscript up until the moment it went to press. For Molly, Rebekah, and Karen, I love you all.

Next, my parents Tony and Jeannie Phillips deserve immeasurable recognition for supporting my ambitions throughout the years and for instilling within me the values of hard work, self-discipline, and high standards. Any accomplishment I may have is because of this upbringing. Finally, I wish to thank my family in Camden, New Jersey, for sharing their lives with me. I especially want to acknowledge the love and wisdom of Ms. Carol, Siddiq, Mr. Billy, Danielle, Mr. Will, Meda, Lawrence, Mr. Charles, Ms. Loretta, Poogie, Pitbull, Gerald, Carlos, Mr. Headley, Micki, Mehregan, Will, and the rest of the crew at Frank's Place. They have influenced and shaped my scholarship more than anyone else. I can only hope that they are proud of the work I've done.

Table of Contents

"Today it is fashionable to talk about
the poor. Unfortunately, it is not
fashionable to talk with them."
—*Mother Teresa*

"Of all the preposterous assumptions of humanity
over humanity, nothing exceeds most of the
criticisms made on the habits of the poor by the
well-housed, well-warmed, and well-fed."
—*Herman Melville*

Preface

In December 2003 I participated in my first week-long volunteer trip as a 19-year-old college sophomore. Along with 10 other people, I spent the week after final exams in Grand Rapids, Michigan, serving meals at a soup kitchen, reading to second graders in a local elementary school, rocking babies at a community daycare center, and handing out blankets to the homeless who were sleeping in the city parks. During this trip, while walking around downtown late one night I met a man named Jeremiah. Jeremiah was homeless and appreciated the blanket, but he wasn't content with just receiving a handout and allowing me to move on to the next person in need. Instead, he turned our encounter into an hour-long question and answer session. "Why are you here?" "What do you know about this area?" "Have you ever been homeless?" "What are you going to do after you leave and I'm still on the streets?" "This blanket is nice, but wouldn't it be better if you got me a hotel room for the night?" Some of his questions were hostile and made me a bit apprehensive, but I welcomed the argument. I faked my way through some self-righteous answers, but the truth was that I was 19, knew nothing about homelessness, and was volunteering because volunteering was "the right thing to do."

Since meeting Jeremiah, I have partaken in numerous other volunteering opportunities and have read countless books on homelessness, poverty, and income inequality. And what I have found over the years is that many of the stories I had heard directly from the homeless living on the streets were not documented anywhere in these books. Most books on the subject speak in generalizations about welfare policy, public housing, and food security. Hardly any spent a significant amount of time capturing the experiences and the narratives of those who are homeless. Some read as if the author had never met a homeless person. While I appreciated reading the books written by economists who crunched the numbers as well as the op-eds written by political pundits who debated government budgets, I was more interested in learning from the homeless firsthand by listening to their stories. Perhaps they had something substantive to say about welfare policy, public housing, and food security. After all, they were the ones most reliant on these systems. That is what this book attempts to do: It centers the experiences of the homeless to better understand the issue of homelessness. Without understanding the experiences of the homeless, all we are left with is a public debate where polarized academics and politicians make theoretical arguments over an issue that none of them ever lived through at ground level.

Notably, I am not homeless, have never been homeless, and am not proposing that this book speaks on behalf of the homeless. This book simply tries to communicate stories of homelessness based on firsthand observations, ethnographic research, and formal interviews. To better capture the experiences of the homeless, this book moves through four parts. Part I recounts my year of volunteering at a local homeless shelter in Camden, New Jersey. Part II summarizes the current scholarship addressing homelessness. Part III presents formal interviews from people who are homeless and living in southern Illinois. Part IV offers implications for policy changes and future research.

Since completing this research, I have presented the findings at a few community events and forums. After an event in Carbondale, Illinois, a local journalist called me for an interview. In a moment of frustration and candor, I finally told her, "Look, it boils down to this: Conservatives tend to ignore the issue and liberals are too infantilizing." The comment was brash and, of course, generalizing, but I still believe the sentiment is accurate. The truth is that homeless people are people and they move through the world with complexities, just like everyone else. Conservatives need to recognize that the problem of homelessness exists and that people who are homeless need public support. Liberals need to recognize that people who are homeless are adults who need to be held accountable for their choices, and that you cannot keep throwing money at a broken system and expect different results. Ultimately, the only way to have any holistic and honest political debate regarding this issue is by making sure the homeless are part of these discussions.

PART I
CAMDEN, NEW JERSEY

1. Introduction

At some point during July of 2006 I found myself standing outside a Duty Free store in the middle of a familiar-looking East Coast airport. Having just returned to the United States from an international trip to Zanzibar, I was tired, in need of a shower, and loaded down with luggage. My traveling companions and I had a couple of hours before our final leg back to Detroit, so we found a comfortable corner to stretch our legs and catch a nap. Like many of those who had traveled with me, I had packed my cell phone, but had not turned it on or checked my messages since I had left the United States two weeks prior. I turned on my phone and began listening to my voicemail. Caught between the usual messages from friends and family was a message from a recruiter with the organization Mission Year.

During the fall semester of 2005, my senior year in college, I had filled out an application to join Mission Year. My friend Erin had done the program two years before I applied and had nothing but positive things to say about her experience. The summary of the program is this: six people live in a house together for a year and volunteer in whatever city they are placed. In exchange for volunteering, the program provides a modest stipend for food and housing. The community standards included no television, no Internet, no personal vehicles, and limited phone calls as well as communal meals, communal reading experiences, and community outreach. One of the reasons for these standards is the idea of "intentional community." Essentially, in order to more fully connect with people you have to make the effort in becoming more fully present and active with those around you.

As I was applying for the Mission Year program, I was also applying to Central Michigan University's Communication graduate program. I knew I wanted to further my education in a field that would allow me to further explore social issues steeped in histories of power

3

and marginalization, but I also wanted the option of leaving the academy for a moment to experience some of these social issues as they were happening in everyday communities. In the end, I decided to defer my graduate school acceptance for a year and accepted a position with Mission Year.

Back at the airport I nervously listened to the recruiter's message. I had already been accepted to the program during the spring of 2006, but I had not been told where I would be living for the next year of my life. When I applied to Mission Year, the options included Oakland, California; Atlanta, Georgia; Philadelphia, Pennsylvania; and Chicago, Illinois. I requested Oakland as my first choice when I received my general acceptance letter a few months prior. First, it was far away and I was already familiar with the three cities in the east. Second, that's where Erin had spent her year, and since she enjoyed it, I figured it was a safe bet.

With all the anticipation and excitement that had been building around the possibility of leaving for Oakland within a matter a weeks, you can imagine the surprise when the voicemail said, "Josh, we have placed you in Camden, New Jersey." Camden, New Jersey? I had never heard of the place and based on the materials Mission Year had sent me, I didn't even know Camden was an option. With no easily accessible Internet access in the airport and no one to call, I shut down my phone with more questions than answers about where I would be spending the next year of my life. Those questions would have to wait until I got back home and could do some research.

In the preface of his book, *Camden After the Fall*, history professor Howard Gillette (2005) captures the familiar feelings that many outsiders have about Camden when he writes:

> Cars passing through [via interstate 676] won't be bothered by the smoke emitted from the stacks. Their drivers won't contemplate the homes displaced or the neighborhoods disrupted to make their commutes easier ... [outsiders] may be stimulated by what they see, but they remain safely distant. What they know—or think they know—of this city assures them that it is best to keep that distance ... [outsiders] have learned through repeated media accounts that the city is not just poor and badly run. It is a dangerous and inhospitable place marked by crime as well as corruption [xii].

These perceptions can be difficult to confront, but they are rooted in real and troublesome data. For example, Camden consistently ranks near the top of the FBI's list of the most dangerous cities in America (Gibson, 2010; Mach, 2012). Additionally, recent census data indicates that 42.5 percent of Camden residents live below the poverty line ("New Census," 2012). Within the abject poverty, a staggering number of homeless people have found themselves bedding down in Camden's transportation center, shelters, and abandoned housing.

(An immediate concern of this research is how to distinguish people and groups through labels. There are valid arguments for always using "person first language" such as "people who are homeless." However, I made the decision to interchangeably use the terms "people who are homeless," "the homeless," and "homeless people" where I felt it enhanced brevity and clarity.)

It is estimated that more than 3,000 homeless people live in Camden County (Volunteers of America Delaware Valley, 2010), many of whom funnel into the city of Camden for services. These types of numbers led Camden to the title of the poorest city in America (Romeo, 2012). With few job prospects for low-skilled workers or the long-term unemployed, a struggling economy, and Camden's high school graduation rate consistently hovering around 50 percent (United States Census Bureau, 2010), I am led to believe that this impoverishment will not end anytime soon.

When I moved to Camden in August of 2006, it fit the profile of everything I had read. Because there is no direct volunteer program established under Mission Year, it is up to each participant to find a local community program to work with during the next 12 months. Most people forego any serious volunteer searching until after they have taken the first week (or two) to settle into their surroundings by moving in, meeting neighbors, and learning the public transportation schedule. I was no different. After about a week I still had no idea where I was going to volunteer. Finally, I met Maxine after a Sunday morning service at New Mickle Baptist Church.

Maxine was an older woman who had lived in and around Camden most of her life. The pastor of the church, the Reverend Allen, had pointed out the six new college-age kids sitting near the back of the church and made sure we felt at home in the congregation. After service, Maxine introduced herself and began asking me about how I planned to serve the community. I told her that I wasn't sure and she prophetically answered, "You're going to end up at New Visions." The next morning at 7:30 a.m., my roommate Will and I made the four-block walk to 523 Stevens Street, New Visions Day Shelter.

For the next 12 months, Will and I would join the staff at New Visions (more commonly known as Frank's Place in remembrance of a deceased homeless man) Monday through Thursday for a four-hour shift. Carved out of the belly of an old decrepit church, Frank's catered to hundreds of people every Monday through Friday, 8:00 a.m.–4:00 p.m. While I was there, the patron list included well over 1,200 names and there were no viable rooms or resources for allowing the shelter to remain open overnight. The daily duties for the staff included organizing the food pantry, organizing the clothing area, cooking breakfast and lunch, managing the showers, washing linens, taking out the trash, and dealing with the chaos of high school volunteers, church groups, and food deliveries. During my time there, I had taken on every assignment at one time or another, but mostly my role involved intake for new clients.

Intake was a demanding task because every day new clients would arrive at the shelter hoping to receive services. In order to receive services, New Visions had a policy of collecting several pages of information on every patron that came through the door. The process was extensive and asked questions on topics ranging from name and address to welfare benefits and medical history. Those who went through the intake process included mothers picking up weekly food bags to take home to their children to homeless men who were only passing through and wanted a hot meal before leaving town. This rather invasive process of collecting such personal information on everyone who came through the door allowed New Visions' executive board to quantify personal data for government grant applications that requested the specific makeup of clientele. The more detailed the grant, the easier it was to quantify services and the more likely it was that an agency would receive additional funding. Between staff members, board members, grant writers, and government agencies that granted funding, there were many people involved in this complex system of counting patrons and shifting money. The only absent voices in this money-shifting conversation were those of the patrons.

⊹╫⊹

The origins of today's methods for government funding of welfare services began roughly 50 years ago and have been expanding exponentially ever since. In the mid–1960s, President Lyndon B. Johnson called upon the United States Congress to begin a national war on poverty and to create the foundation for what would become known as Johnson's "Great Society" legislation. In all, this legislation was aimed at creating upward mobility for those most vulnerable to the grip of poverty, including the lower-class and homeless populations. However, today we are nearly a half-century removed from the beginnings of this war and the poverty rates remain unchanged (Blackwell, 2012; Murray, 2012; see Murray, 1984; Smiley & West, 2012). Countless scholars and politicians have theorized why poverty and homelessness rates remain stagnant, but little research has been done that directly poses questions of economic and social policy to those most affected by homelessness. Therefore, the purpose of this book is to provide a space in which to engage with those individuals facing homelessness, in an effort to fashion better-functioning economic and social policies for those most invested in the outcomes. In doing so, this book will create an academic account of homelessness that is inspired by the experiences of those who live these vulnerable realities each and every day.

Since leaving Camden, I still remain close to several people I met at the shelter and have since worked and volunteered at other shelters outside Camden. As an advocate closely connected to the issue of homelessness, it is easy to make demands aimed at increasing government funding for a plethora of poverty programs. Essentially, "I want my friends who are homeless to live more comfortably, so give them more money." However, as a scholar deeply committed to *ending* homelessness—as opposed to simply *managing* homelessness—I have recently found myself engaging with this issue through more critical lines of questioning. Perhaps most contentious is my academic certainty that pouring more money into broken systems will not solve the problem. In fact, increased spending on certain government programs might actually impede progress or even exacerbate the problem. To this end, I have come to the conclusion that money is neither the root problem nor the foundational solution when confronting homelessness. Instead, access to money is simply a symptom of a larger cultural problem and government funding is simply used as a Band-Aid to try and cover up much larger issues. As a replacement for the money argument, this book argues that homelessness exists and homelessness rates remain stagnant because our society is culturally divided between those who have homes and those who do not. Essentially, how can politicians, academics, and social workers know what types of social, political, and welfare programs will drive down the rate of homelessness if homeless people aren't being asked about their current experiences within these programs? Therefore, it is important to listen to the voices of the homeless as their stories can help policymakers better understand the culture of homelessness and consequently, advocate for social, political, and welfare programs that will actually be beneficial in helping the homeless obtain financial independence and long-term housing.

2. Frank's Place

In late–August 2006, I moved into a house with five strangers. Our home was located on the 300 block of Clinton Street. This two-story row house was complete with paper-thin indoor wooden paneling, a light blue painted-concrete exterior, and iron bars covering the windows. These bars are common in many urban neighborhoods to prevent break-ins, but they also serve as a way to make people feel trapped in their own home. Outside these bars, crime is prevalent and unpredictable. It's better to be locked inside one's home after dark.

This downtown address was within walking distance of the Walter Rand Transportation Center, the Camden Waterfront, and a basketball court. Since we arrived in August, students could be found at the basketball court every day soaking up their last few weeks of summer freedom. In an effort to meet people and learn more about the area, a few of us frequently visited the courts and conversed with other spectators sitting in the bleachers. At first, our presence was met with skepticism. Conversations were mostly hesitant nods of recognition and dodgy answers to basic questions. This was a tight-knit community leery of outsiders, especially young white men. To break the ice and build some trust, our house pooled together what little money we had and bought a cooler, two bags of ice, and several cases of Gatorade. On a 90-degree day in early September, we walked to the courts with the supplies. We handed out Gatorade to the teenagers on the court and were finally allowed to speak with the adults in the stands.

"Keith" (in addition to the pseudonyms given to the interviewees in Part III, many other names have been changed) was the court's patriarch. He knew all the players, coached both teams, and was allowed to interrupt the game for whatever reason: timeouts, coaching, or even discipline. He was also our most generous source of information once he found out that we were connected with New Mickle Baptist Church.

9

"You can't come around here unless you're connected to someone in the neighborhood," he would say. We would later find out that the initial skepticism of our presence was because people thought we were undercover cops trying to glean information. After all, cops were pretty much the only white people interested in speaking to people in this neighborhood and, with the high-rate of violent crime, most cops weren't there to make friends. The leeriness was justified.

Walter Rand Transportation Center

The initial suspicion extended into every social circle we entered and working with the homeless was no different. While dozens of people within the homeless community knew Will and me from working at Frank's Place, many were cautious about interacting with us outside the shelter. Similar to undercover cops looking for clues by striking up casual conversations in the neighborhood, social workers sometimes checked up on their clients in less formal settings to monitor progress. While addicts and hustlers could stay clean for a few early morning hours to utilize shelter services, at some point in the late afternoon they had to feed the addiction. Will and I had no interest in monitoring clients' late-night behaviors nor would either one of us pass judgment on those who did wrestle with addiction. All we wanted was to build community, meet needs, and exhibit love to those whose humanity is sometimes questioned and too often dismissed.

When Frank's Place closed every day at 4:00 p.m., people scattered. Within a couple of hours, some would end up at a night shelter that held a few dozen cots, but this was nowhere near enough beds for the entire homeless population of Camden. Others squatted in abandoned buildings throughout the city. And with a 1 in 12 vacancy rate, there were more than enough acceptable houses to choose from. However, shacking up in a vacant house was not without risks. For example, every window and door was boarded up. While this added layer of confinement may have kept others from recognizing one's illegal squatting, it also meant that no one was monitoring the house in case of an emergency or violent crime: e.g., fire, overdose, assault, murder, or rape. If one decided to live in a vacant, he or she was isolated from the usual neighborly surveillance and police assistance. Living in a vacant assumed complete self-protection. When shelters were filled and vacants too risky, a third option was to sleep outside. For many of Camden's homeless, this meant sleeping at the Walter Rand Transportation Center. The transportation center is a large hub that connects south Jersey's public transportation to Pennsylvania's SEPTA system. It also has a rail line to north Jersey and buses into NYC and other big cities. To the untraveled homeless, the benefit of this space is that it spans multiple buildings, is located in downtown Camden, well-lit, warm, and has enough foot traffic to feel safe at night.

After working at Frank's Place for about a month, Will and I wanted to connect with people on a more personal level. Thus far, our work in Camden had mostly consisted of cataloguing clients, clothing, food, and services. We really didn't know anybody beyond these statistics and everyday politeness, so we decided to meet up with people outside of work. The first step was to start visiting the transportation center a few times per week at around 8:00 p.m. when people began shuffling into the smaller building on the west side of Broadway. Like our initial introductions to neighbors at the basketball courts, it was difficult to get the conversations started. Luckily for us, there was a Dunkin' Donuts inside the main building that was open 24 hours and sold doughnuts for half-price after 6:00 p.m. Similar to our plan with the Gatorade, we began purchasing two dozen doughnuts a few times per week and handing them out to people.

Our biggest supporter in these efforts was a guy named Mase. Mase was a Vietnam vet with a slim build, dark skin, large eyes, and long dreadlocks. He also had a habit of wearing all of his clothes at once so he wouldn't lose anything. It wasn't uncommon to see him in five coats and three pairs of pants while sweat pooled above the creases in his weathered face. He hung out near the Dunkin' Donuts every day asking for change so he could buy coffee and a snack. While our budget was tight (only $60 per month, per person in extra spending money) we always added a "Mase special" onto our order anytime he was around: a large coffee with cream and sugar and a plain bagel with strawberry cream cheese.

With Mase satisfied, we offered the doughnuts to others lingering outside the transportation center late at night. Not everyone who partook was homeless. Some of the people we met were simply catching a bus to work third-shift at a factory in the suburbs. Some were just

11

looking for a safe place to walk around at night after a family fight at home. And a few had just gotten out of Camden County Jail and were waiting for the bus to take them back to wherever was home. The recently released inmates were probably the most excited about Dunkin' Donuts, especially Jack. After eating jail food for the past six months, he began jumping and yelling after biting into a delicious chocolate doughnut. To this bald-headed tough guy covered in demon tattoos, nothing tasted this good. He ended up grabbing two more by placing them on his fingers like rings and ate them in quick succession.

Once inside the smaller building of the transportation center, we cracked open the boxes and ate the remaining doughnuts with people we knew were staying in for the night. This usually consisted of a group of about eight people who had developed a support system with one another. They shared resources and watched each other's belongings. One guy, Chuck, even had a radio for community entertainment. Throughout the fall, we would sit around and eat doughnuts while listening to football games. Most of the people listening to those games had to struggle through the year as disappointed Eagles fans, while I had a great time cheering on the Bears all the way to the Super Bowl.

As time passed, relationships grew stronger and we found ourselves arriving at the transportation center earlier in the evenings just to have extra time for conversations. However, by late November, other commitments to the neighborhood were piling up and we were only able to visit the transportation center once a week. So there was a rush to get down there early on our nights off and catch up on everything that had been happening in the past week. After this routine went on for a couple of months, small talk and doughnuts just didn't cut it anymore. These were no longer just homeless people looking for spare change, charitable gestures, and polite conversations; these were friends who had real lives, real families, and real dreams. And friends get invited over for dinner.

Fortunately, as a house, the six of us had made a commitment to host hospitality dinners once a week. On Tuesday nights, people were invited over from all areas of our lives: work, church, neighborhood, afterschool program, family, visiting friends, and the shelter. It was a recurring invite with a constantly evolving guest list, and we always seemed to have enough food. On more than one occasion, people who were homeless would stop by for a meal before finding shelter for the night. On at least one occasion, I drove our 15-person passenger van around downtown to pick people up for dinner when it was too cold to walk. Most of the people picked up were people I knew, but there were also those I didn't know who just wanted some company and a hot meal. While picking up strangers and bringing them home might not be the safest idea, this was a house where six college-aged people lived and it was filled with several others every Tuesday night. The worst that could have happened was someone stealing a book from our living room shelves.

During one evening, a homeless woman named Genevieve was thumbing through the books to no particular ends. We chatted about some of the titles and authors. She was familiar with a few famous American authors such as Mark Twain and John Steinbeck, but English was her second language and she couldn't recall having access to many Spanish translations growing up in Puerto Rico. What really interested her on the bookshelf, however, was an empty notebook. She asked if she could rip a few blank pages out of the notebook because she needed the paper to write some letters. I gave her the entire notebook and told her she could return the remaining paper to me once the letters had been written.

A week later Genevieve stopped by my office at the shelter to return the paper and ask for a few envelopes and stamps. I had the envelopes, but no stamps. She wrote down the addresses and I offered to drop them off at the post office later that day where I'd be able to purchase stamps. Before sealing the envelopes she asked me to proof-read the letters because of her broken English. Each letter read well, but there was one glaring item that caught my attention. To begin, one of the letters was a plea to a housing authority asking for help with rent. Apparently, Genevieve's application for an apartment had been accepted, but she couldn't obtain the full down payment so she was asking to move in with a promise to pay the remainder of the down payment over the next several months. While these negotiations are not unusual, what stuck out in this letter was the way she described her current living conditions. Throughout the letter, she continuously made reference to the transportation center as her current residence. There was no mention of "homelessness" or "shelter," but an ongoing discussion about her day-to-day activities *living* at the transportation center. For instance, she wrote, "I currently live at the Walter Rand Transportation Center ... there are no beds here and I have to share the building with lots of other people.... I am almost 60-years-old and need a place to myself."

Unfortunately for Genevieve and everyone else living at the Walter Rand Transportation Center, they were about to get evicted. Just before Christmas 2006, the Camden, New Jersey City Council, police department, and transportation authority closed the indoor portions of the transportation center's west building. The building was fine, the lights were left on, and you could still see inside seating thanks to the floor-to-ceiling windows, but the doors were bolted shut and large accordion gates were placed just inside the glass. That way, if anyone had any ideas about breaking the locks, the gates were there as a second barrier to block access. I asked a late-night security guard why they had closed the building. Perhaps the building was slotted for construction, an addition, demolition, or had been condemned for violating some code? But none of these explanations were true. In his unofficial answer, the security guard explained that Camden wanted to attract more visitors downtown and it couldn't do that if visitors were greeted by a transportation center lobby full of homeless people. Notably, there was, and remains, an ongoing revitalization effort along the Delaware River that includes an aquarium, baseball stadium, music amphitheater, waterfront walkway, several parks, Rutgers University, and Cooper Hospital. Apparently, a shuttered lobby was a better visual for welcoming tourists than having to pass by a few rugged homeless people sleeping on benches and asking for spare change.

Even though the lobby was off-limits, the transportation center remained the safest place for a homeless person to sleep in Camden. The only difference was that people were now sleeping outside in the middle of December instead of sleeping in a heated lobby. There were city regulations that allowed for emergency shelter when the temperature dropped below a certain degree. During these times, several public buildings would open in the middle of the night and shuttle people indoors. But these nights were the exceptions. Besides, if inclement weather is defined as "below freezing," then that doesn't do a lot of good for the people sleeping outside when it's 35 degrees out.

We continued to make doughnut runs after the lobby had been boarded up, but the atmosphere had changed. People had dispersed and there was less cohesion. Some continued to sleep near the transportation center while others retreated to secluded areas of local parks or made their way into the vacants. Now, instead of sitting down and listening to the radio with 10 people, our conversations were more one-on-one. However awful this new arrangement was with regard to weather, privacy, and monitoring, there was a silver lining. In short, the absence of one large group compelled us to develop more personal relationships. During this stretch, I became close with a man named Mr. Lawrence, whom I had known since my first week in Camden. He was soft-spoken and purposeful. Even though his labor wasn't required at the shelter, he always managed to find a broom and dustpan. He liked to contribute, he liked to work, and he liked order. His philosophy was that all people, even those with meager means, should strive for cleanliness and devotion to one's work.

In mid–January 2007, I met up with Mr. Lawrence on a particularly cold night. He was bundled up in two sleeping bags and pressed against the outside doors of the transportation center. Because of the weather, Will and I opted to purchase hot chocolate and coffee instead of doughnuts. After passing out the hot beverages, Will walked to a nearby parking lot to meet with a friend and I stayed behind with Mr. Lawrence. It was still relatively early, about 9:00 p.m., but Mr. Lawrence was already hunkered down with the sleeping bags pulled over his face to keep the light out. I asked if I could join him, and with his usual generosity he unfolded part of his sleeping bags so I wouldn't have to rest on the cold concrete. I laid down next to him and for several moments we just stared up at the night sky. The view was impressive. Though we were surrounded by the city, all of the buildings, artificial lights, noise, politics, and problems seemed to disappear. Finally, Mr. Lawrence broke the silence and in his calm, reassuring voice said, "You know Josh, just remember, it's a big sky up there." It sure is Mr. Lawrence. It sure is.

Tent City

Besides the transportation center, the other large gathering spot for people sleeping outside was a place known as Tent City. Tent cities exist in many communities with sizable homeless populations and

Camden was no different. Throughout the past several years I have visited multiple Tent City locations across the United States and have found that many of them are located on the outskirts of town and hidden within a small forest of trees or amongst long-abandoned former industrial areas. However, what was unique about Camden's Tent City was its ability to remain concealed right in the middle of such a populated area. The entrance to Tent City was located along the heavily trafficked Route 30 and was nestled behind overgrown brush below an overpass. Thousands of motorists drove within 20 feet of this location every day and were none-the-wiser about its existence. The amount of people living in Tent City fluctuated, but there was enough infrastructure to accommodate upwards of 30 people. Because many people treated this space as a home, they were wary of outside visitors. This was where people kept their belongings, let their guard down, and experienced community. Unknown outsiders threatened this balance.

While I knew several of the people who called Tent City home, I didn't enter Tent City until after seven months of working at Frank's. The delayed visit was mainly due to a few people's demeanor who were self-conscious about their living conditions. No one had outright denied access. After all, it was a public space that was easily accessible. But when the topic of Tent City came up, some people became tentative and cautious about disclosing too many details. The discomfort was apparent. They knew me in a professional setting at Frank's, but were concerned about the enormous vulnerability that came with exposing the squalor that accompanied a life spent living in a small field next to the highway.

When I finally did visit, it was with permission. I had met up with two of Tent City's residents on Saturday afternoon for lunch at a downtown McDonald's. They had several bags of clothing and food they had received from a local Catholic charity and asked if I could help them carry the items home. Tent City was only a short walk east, so I agreed. The entrance was a narrow path that wound through some tall grasses, so there was no direct line of sight from the road. Even though a few scattered pieces of plywood were strategically placed over large holes and divots, the path was mostly mud from the previous day's rain. As I watched my steps to avoid getting my shoes too dirty, I couldn't help but notice that small baggies and broken syringes were littered every-

16

where and had been pressed deeply into the ground from the constant in and out traffic of residents.

At the end of the path, the area opened like a large meadow. Until now, the tall grasses had obstructed any view that would have given some sense of size and makeup. However, standing at the edge of the clearing, I estimated the established area was a good 60 feet in diameter. Within this boundary was a rudimentary encampment with all the basic necessities for survival. There were approximately six shelters composed of plywood frames and tarp roofs. The shelters were impressively large and could have easily fit 5–6 people per unit. In the middle of Tent City was a fire pit with a few grills and pots for cooking as well as a kettle for making coffee. Since it was still relatively chilly in mid–March, the kettle was currently hung above the fire heating yesterday's brew. Dispersed between the shelters and the fire pit was a large collection of salvaged furniture. There were lawn chairs, futons, end tables, coffee tables, couches, and hammocks. There was such an abundant amount of furniture that many pieces were simply discarded after the cushions were repeatedly soaked and then rotted out during stormy weather. Like the rest of the trash, this rotting furniture was thrown into the large garbage piles that encircled most of the encampment.

On the opposite side of the entrance was a collection of five-gallon buckets and a standalone plastic wall that created a privacy barrier between the main camp and the small restroom situated on the edge of the brush. This may have helped create some sense of privacy, but it did very little to cut down on the area's overall stench. In no uncertain terms, the place was filthy. While people did their best to keep the middle of camp clean, the place was still surrounded by piles of garbage with no means for trash removal. On a daily basis, people brought in items such as food, clothing, toiletries, household items, and furniture. Unfortunately, no one took away these items once they had been used. Instead, people just threw them into the brush until the garbage pile became unmanageable. This setup attracted dozens of feral cats who roamed freely within Tent City picking through old Crown Fried Chicken boxes and catching the occasional mouse. Tent City was a health hazard to its residents, the cats, and the larger Camden community. Yet even among all this garbage, the far bigger health concern within Tent City was the rampant drug use and strewn paraphernalia.

17

Candy and Biscuits

Camden is a 24/7 open-air drug market. Just outside the shelter was a dealer named James shouting out "candy and biscuits" every morning for anyone interested in procuring some dope. At first, dealers like James approached me daily to see if I was looking to buy. Truth be told, the main reason any college-aged white kid came into this neighborhood was to buy. Rutgers University Camden was only a few blocks up the street, and it was common to see a nice car full of white kids roll through our neighborhood to make a quick purchase. In fact, one block over from our house was a little mom-and-pop operation that sold drugs right off the front porch. And without fail, every Friday afternoon a pristine silver Mustang full of white college students pulled up to the curb, made an exchange through the car window, and drove off with no regard for the children and the families living in our neighborhood.

The pervasive cash flow from white Rutgers students was so bad that Will and I once got stopped by the police at *8 o'clock in the morning* on a Tuesday while walking to work. Just outside New Mickle Baptist Church, Will and I were about to turn east up Stevens Street when a patrol car flew up behind us, slammed on its brakes, and flipped on its lights. "What are you two doing down here?" the officer hollered. I told him that we were on our way to work, but he didn't believe it. He followed up with several more questions about where we worked, where we lived, for how long, and a few detail-oriented questions meant to trip us up. After some back and forth bickering, he decided to let us go "with a warning" and cautioned us about the dangers of walking around this neighborhood.

There were several more incidents throughout the year where police arbitrarily questioned us about possible drug purchasing, and I don't share these stories as some sort of righteous statement against police profiling "young white men" in Camden. That would be absurd and wildly indecorous. However, these experiences illuminate the reality that the drug-related demise of some inner-city neighborhoods does not exist in a vacuum. The reason I was stopped more frequently in Camden than during any other time in my life was because so many young white people came into this neighborhood to buy drugs. If white America wants to thumb its nose at communities of color for allowing drug dealers to run inner-city corners, then white America needs to

18

first start by condemning all those white college students getting high on daddy's allowance.

For its part, Frank's Place was vigilant about keeping drugs and weapons out of the shelter. There was a strict "no tolerance" policy that was ruthlessly enforced. A single pill or mundane pocketknife was enough to garner a 90-day suspension: no questions asked. A second offense was at least a year-long suspension and sometimes more depending on the severity. To monitor the hundreds of clients that came through daily, Frank's essentially eliminated all forms of privacy. For example, there were separate men's and women's bathrooms, but all the doors to the stalls had been removed. Previous to removing the doors, people would sometimes shoot up dope in the stalls and then fallout or overdose while locked inside. The worst case scenario was that a person overdosed and remained propped on the toilet. In these instances, a person's emergency medical needs could go unnoticed for several minutes. It was always best if they fell to the floor or made a loud noise falling against the wall so that someone would notice. When an overdose did happened, staff would either have to drag the person out from under the stalls or break down the door. The prospect of spending time and money to replace doors was frustrating for the staff and the ordeal of being dragged across a bathroom floor was unsanitary for the clients. The lesser of two evils was to remove the doors and forego normal restroom privacy, however awkward it may be.

In addition to shelter staff, the police and government caseworkers also monitored drug abuse within Camden's homeless population. The police were known for tracking down criminals, who sometimes hid out among the homeless, by vigilantly monitoring the shelter's foot traffic through increased police cruisers and hidden street cameras. About once every two weeks, police did a sweep through the shelter looking for suspects and others with outstanding warrants. Of course, this put everyone on edge. For one, if a suspect was present, no one knew how he or she would react to being arrested. Things could quickly get out of control and in a relatively small space of several dozen people, chaos could ensue. Secondly, the police didn't always announce who they were looking for. So, for some clients with criminal histories, they got nervous around police because they didn't know if they were getting locked up.

Government appointed caseworkers, on the other hand, usually dealt with drug abuse through less aggressive means. This typically entailed a regular drug screening for people on parole. Of course, if people didn't show up for their screenings, then the police would get involved. But this was hardly necessary. Mainly because it was fairly easy to cheat the tests. If a urine test was required, people could easily sneak clean urine into the facility by simply taping a vial to their leg. Truth be told, there aren't too many caseworkers who are overly zealous about searching for stale urine on a parolee. Overall, the urine test is fairly quick and doesn't involve a lot of a one-on-one interaction. However, if a parolee had to interact with a caseworker beyond a urine test, then hiding one's addiction could be a little trickier. This was especially true for people who used needles, since track marks and scars were rampant on their arms and it was easy to determine the freshness of an injection. To avoid detection, people who used needles began to shoot-up in less visible areas. More commonly, this meant injecting dope in between the webbing of one's toes or through the webbing of one's hands. In searching for more prominent veins, there were also those who injected drugs into their genitals and a few men who utilized veins in their necks that could be hidden behind a beard.

It should go without saying, but it's worth mentioning that a lot of people who are addicts know they're addicts, are ashamed of their situation, and want to get sober. Behind defensive posturing and denial are real people who are acutely aware of the reckless and dangerous lifestyle surrounding them. Even if they are unwilling to articulate their dependency to friends and family, in quiet moments of solitude they reflect on their vulnerability. It's not as if these individuals dreamed of growing up, becoming homeless, and living out of a crack house. This is not to say that drug addicts hold no responsibility for their choices. They do. However, these choices were made within specific contexts and influenced by specific cultural factors.

As my time in Camden pressed on, I was privileged to hear some people openly talk about their addictions. Marvin was a 50-year-old current addict who regularly took time to speak with the groups of high school and college volunteers who would stop by Frank's Place every few weeks for a weekend of volunteer service. Unlike professional speakers who were *former* addicts, Marvin spoke against drugs while still in the midst of his demons. Dressed in tattered tank tops and stained jeans, he talked about how he started using marijuana in high school.

Before he knew it, he began lacing the marijuana with stronger drugs because the mellow high wasn't enough. Marvin acknowledged the life he wasted and "accepted the fact" that he would "always be an addict." He had no plans to quit and openly told groups of volunteers that he was going to get high that night. At this stage in his life and with so much talent squandered, he thought the only legacy he could leave behind was a dire warning. Marvin hadn't taken care of himself. Now he constantly worried about the new generation of young people who were going to experiment with drugs and then "wake up in 30 years" not knowing how they ended up living on the streets.

Threats and Violence

Even though Camden was recognized as the Most Dangerous City in America during the time I lived there, there were some areas within the city that were relatively safe to walk through late at night: the walk home from the transportation center, a walk to the waterfront, or a walk around Rutgers campus. Since members of our household regularly relied on public transportation, it wasn't unusual to walk around these areas of Camden long after dark. This was especially true during the winter months when the sun was setting around 5:00 p.m. With no television or Internet distractions available, one can't expect six college-aged people to just sit around every night in a two-bedroom, one-bathroom house and not feel claustrophobic. You can only read so many books and play so many card games. On other nights, you just need space. While I mostly remained vigilant with regard to personal safety, there were nights when terrible and stupid decisions were made. Perhaps none as stupid as the time Will and I visited a vacant.

The story of our journey into the vacant begins with a woman named LaKeesha. LaKeesha was a 27-year-old homeless woman who was seven months pregnant and had a fierce heroin addiction. Her first child had already been taken away from her by the state and Child Protective Services was aggressively monitoring her current situation because of the pregnancy. When she did go into labor, social services would be at her bedside just waiting to take the newborn baby away from her: no questions asked. Her boyfriend Al was a 40-year-old former drug dealer who did what he could to protect the unborn child from LaKeesha's habit, but there were times when she would disappear for days and Al could only assume that she was using. For those who worked at the shelter, we did what we could to support LaKeesha with fresh clothes, nutritious meals, and personal hygiene products, but there was nothing the staff could do to help her once the shelter closed at 4:00 p.m.

In a moment of 22-year-old naiveté, I thought it would helpful to make sure that she and Al were at least provided dinners until the baby was born. Frank's Place only served breakfast and lunch and I had seen how hungry people were by 8:00 o'clock at night when passing out doughnuts at the transportation center. LaKeesha always had a small bag of food that she carried around, but she had no way of cooking the dry pasta or warming the cold soup. Will and I agreed to help by preparing the food and then delivering it later that evening.

LaKeesha and Al lived in a familiar vacant a few blocks from our house. It was an old six-story apartment building where at least a dozen other homeless people slept every night. The building was solid, the rooms were private, and enough furniture had been left behind to make the place relatively comfortable for squatters. Given its proximity to Rutgers and the fact that we had arrived at 7:00 p.m., it seemed safe enough to enter. We made our way up a back alley to where a board hung dislodged in front of a first-floor window. On the other side of the window was a toilet and complete darkness. We took a few steps into an empty bedroom hoping our eyes would adjust to a possible sliver of light through a crack in the wall, but there was no light coming through. All of sudden, a rattling from the bathroom startled us. Someone else was here. "Hello? Do you have a light?" we asked. A man holding a dying matchstick stumbled through the bathroom doorway. He had been following us. He asked a few questions and then demanded money. We didn't have anything, but told him that if he helped us with the light we'd find a way to pay him $5. He agreed.

He crumbled up some newspaper on the ground, shoved it into a piece of cardboard that he had fashioned into a cone, and lit the paper on fire. Then he ran. LaKeesha and Al lived at the end of the hallway on the third floor and we had to move quickly if we were going to get there before the fire burned out. Within an instant, all five of us were in their makeshift living room. There was no electricity, but the room was well-lit. Al had removed the boards covering the windows and light from the streetlamps poured in. LaKeesha took the bag of Tupperware containing the cooked pasta and heated soup and warmly said, "Thank you." All she and Al had eaten since lunch were a few crackers and some potato chips.

Al and the man who had led us upstairs just stared at each other. They vaguely knew each other from around town and the man made Al nervous. Within seconds of arriving, it was clearly time to go. Will and I began to leave, but the man stood in front of the door and asked for payment. "You said you'd give me $10. Now I want my money!" We had only agreed to $5 and reiterated the fact that we currently had nothing on us. He would have to stop by Frank's Place tomorrow to pick it up. But the man was unfazed. He simply moved closer until I could feel his breath yelling in my face. As he continued to rant, he removed a foot long section of a metal tow chain from his pocket and wrapped it around his knuckles. The man was high, agitated, and unpredictable. Al immediately jumped in and tried to calm the situation. He gently grabbed the man by the shoulders, told him that he would get the money he was promised, and then told Will and me to leave. Without light we made our way downstairs and back to the open window by memory and feel. By the time we exited it was only a quarter after seven. After clearing the alley, we turned to see the man climbing out of the bathroom window. Al had held him back to give us a five-minute head start. Even though nothing violent had happened, it was enough to keep me out of the vacants.

While that was the only time I ever felt personally threatened while working with the homeless, there were plenty of instances where I witnessed the aftermath of violence. As a person in charge of client intake, it was common to see people come in to Frank's with bumps and bruises from being robbed and assaulted the night before. Sadly, many of the people who had experienced violence talked about it nonchalantly. For them, violence was normal and expected. It was part of living on the street and everyone had to encounter it at some point.

One woman's casual tone about violence stood in such stark contrast to the details of her intensely jarring story that I repeatedly asked for certain specifics just to make sure that I heard her correctly. Sandra came to the shelter on an unusually warm day in early spring 2007. She had long dyed red hair that was unkempt and showed nearly two inches of her natural brunette roots. Because of the weather, Sandra wore a spaghetti-strap tank top that bared her emaciated arms that were covered in bruises, track marks, and cigarette burns. It was common for pimps to put out cigarettes on girls as a form of punishment. As we worked through the intake process, questions were asked about various health concerns and medications. Sandra conveyed knowledge about a few STDs, but was hesitant in offering assurance that this list was complete. Her appeal for further testing was based on the fact that she had been gang-raped the night before by "three or four … maybe five guys." The tone with which she relayed this information was so incredibly matter-of-fact that I twice asked for clarification about the date of the incident. It seemed impossible that her demeanor remained so serene a mere 12 hours after the incident. After Sandra had completed the intake process, she took a shower, received fresh clothing, and ate a breakfast of bran flakes and coffee. By noon she was on her way to the free health clinic for the morning-after pill and antibiotics.

While women may have been at a greater risk for sexual assault, men were also sometimes victimized. And because, on average, men possess greater size and strength, predators usually have to expend a greater amount of violence in order to subdue male victims. In one instance, a male victim was so badly beaten during a sexual assault, that the shelter staff immediately bought him a bus ticket out of town. The man had been targeted by a group of corner boys in the middle of the night while he slept under the Ben Franklin Bridge in north Camden. He showed up to Frank's the next morning; his clothes stained in blood. He was so overwhelmed with emotion that he could barely speak. A few staff members pulled him into an office where he could have some privacy. Once inside, the man stripped down to his underwear to showcase the violence that had been inflicted on him. His hair had been pulled out, his face was swollen, and bruises and cuts encased his body from being beaten with glass bottles. There was no understandable motive for the crime other than a few young criminals looking to send a violent message and perhaps gain some notoriety through sexual humiliation. After all, the man was homeless. He had no money and no possessions of value. To these criminals, his only worth was in subjugation.

Notably, when violence happened within the homeless community, people found refuge at the shelter. Frank's may have been chaotic, short on resources, and full of addicts and ex-felons, but between 8:00 a.m.

and 4:00 p.m. people were welcomed into a safe environment where they could let their guard down and just be themselves. The worst thing that ever happened was a brief shouting match over whose turn it was in the shower line. One of the most illustrative ways Frank's reputation of safety was made evident was through the ease with which effeminate men freely expressed themselves within the shelter's walls. As one might imagine, living on the streets can be a brutal existence where people are often taken advantage of mentally, physically, and emotionally. As within many communities, homeless or otherwise, effeminate men are oftentimes stereotyped as weak and thus, targeted for exploitation. Therefore, in order to survive, it is imperative that men project traditional masculine qualities.

This type of persona-adjusting was no more evident than in a man named Patrick. Patrick was a six-foot-tall African American man with a vibrant personality. Patrick was also bisexual and preferred to wear women's clothing. In his younger days, he tried to be "out and proud," but after several violent encounters, including assault, robbery, rape, and contracting HIV, Patrick had decided it was best to keep his preferences hidden. Outside of Frank's, Patrick simply had to blend in with every other black man walking down Broadway. However, inside of Frank's, Patrick spent most of his time trying on women's dresses and high-heels. In his backpack he kept a few different-colored wigs, jewelry, purses, and makeup. His name was still Patrick and he spoke in the same voice, but now the clothing was much more comfortable. There were some who were noticeably baffled by Patrick's eccentric choices, but most people didn't care about his sophistications one way or another. Here, Patrick was more than tolerated. He was accepted. Every once-in-a-while a smart-mouth newcomer would make a bigoted joke or complain to the Executive Director, Ms. Sharron, that she shouldn't condone his behavior. But her response was always the same: "This is the one place he can be himself. So just leave him alone."

Crime and Justice

Unfortunately, when violence is committed within the homeless community, people do not always seek help from local law enforcement. While the "no snitching" culture of many inner-city neighborhoods is partially to blame, there is also the fear that an accuser will be arrested by the police for unrelated offenses. For example, a person cannot report a theft of personal property if that property was stolen out of a vacant that the victim was squatting in illegally. In Camden, and increasingly in other communities, there is additional concern over one's immigration status. Camden has a substantial Spanish-speaking Latino population; some of whom are not legal residents of the United States. When a crime is committed against a person who resides in the U.S. illegally, victims are more likely to remain silent than risk deportation.

In lieu of perceived access to the criminal justice system, some people take matters into their own hands. This type of mentality was true for my friend Rico. Rico had a productive background in agriculture work and spent the first few years of his adult life living in the Midwest. He moved to the East Coast 20 years ago to be with family and soon got caught up in inner-city temptations. By the time we met, Rico had been in and out of jail multiple times for minor offenses—mostly shoplifting and drug possession. He never did more than a few weeks in jail at any given time and a day didn't go by when he didn't talk about returning to the farm. But at 45 years old his body was too broken for manual labor and he felt too old for any big changes. It was best to stay with what he knew.

Even though Rico's criminal record was relatively negligible and he was a legal resident, he never could secure above-board work. Frankly, finding employment in and around Camden was hard enough for any job seeker. With so many applications for so few jobs, employers rarely took chances on anyone with a record. They didn't need the risk. So Rico was forced to pick up whatever short-term day labor opportunities were available: landscaping, carpentry, residential moving. On a few rare occasions, Rico and several other people from Frank's would get hired to help clean up the tailgating mess left behind in the parking lots and parks outside the Tweeter Center after a music concert. Because all of his work was under-the-table, Rico got to enjoy compensation that was tax-free and paid in cash. However, this also meant that during a busy week Rico sometimes carried around a few hundred dollars.

Predictably, small amounts of his money had started to go missing on a few separate occasions in a relatively short amount of time, though never through a violent robbery. Rico was a decent-sized man with an attitude that no one wanted to mess with. But over the course of a month, Rico discovered that $20-$30 mysteriously disappeared from his backpack every now and again. At first he figured he had either misplaced it in his jean pockets or a few bills had fallen out while he packed and unpacked his clothing several times a day. Rico attempted to solve this dilemma by sewing a small pocket into the lining of his backpack that would be used to store all his cash. The only way anyone could have found that pocket was by emptying his entire backpack and running their hands inside the lining looking for abnormalities. After the pocket had been sewn and small amounts of money continued to go missing, Rico knew there was a thief in his inner-circle.

Before long, Rico got word that his friend Jeff was showing a little extra cash. Jeff was a dope fiend who mostly kept to himself. To support his habit he usually panhandled for spare change or bartered unused bus tickets he found around the transportation center. When he suddenly stopped scraping together cash and instead just loafed around the campsite all day, people grew suspicious. Rico confronted Jeff, but there was no proof of his indiscretion. It was assumed that the little money he had allegedly stolen went directly to drugs that were immediately consumed. With no cash, no drugs, and no legal recourse for recovering the couple hundred dollars he had lost over several weeks, Rico decided to administer his own form of justice. During the argument, Rico pulled a penknife, stabbed Jeff in the shoulder, and made a small cut on his cheek. Jeff's belongings were tossed and he was banished from the small clique. He now had to face homelessness alone.

Obviously there were elevated dangers faced when someone went through homelessness alone in Camden. For instance, a solitary existence meant that a person was more likely to be targeted for assault and robbery. While sleeping on the streets of Camden was dangerous under any circumstance, sleeping in a small group at least allowed people to either sleep in shifts or sleep in a formation so no one's back was exposed to danger. Conceivably, the biggest advantage of living in a group was that people took notice when someone disappeared. When a disappearance did happen, panic ensued almost instantaneously because there was no real positive reason as to why someone would leave an encampment without prior notice. People may leave for things such as work, rehab, or family visits, but these trips were planned and discussed. When someone simply disappeared without notice, it usually meant they were helpless or dead: frozen in the weather, overdosed, or

27

murdered. During my time in Camden, all three of these things happened and it usually took a couple of weeks to locate the body, identify the victim, and get word back to the shelter. So when one of the most well-known and beloved workers at Frank's went missing for a few weeks in spring 2007, people began to worry.

Akeem was a homeless man who worked the showers and laundry services at Frank's. Like Akeem's duties, almost every task around the shelter was performed on a voluntary basis and most of the people who performed the tasks were homeless. This included the cooks, custodians, food pantry organizers, clothing distributors, people who answered the phones, and people who tracked services. Since none of these positions were funded, the Executive Director found ways to slip a few dollars into the pockets of the regular workers who really kept the shelter moving smoothly. On average, it only amounted to $20 a week for about six different people, but it was the best system available given the enormous need and marginal resources.

Since Akeem's station was right inside the front door and his services were in such high-demand, everyone knew him. Though, when he first went missing, no one paid it too much thought. His girlfriend Porsha substituted for him at his stations and since she wasn't worried, people figured that he must be okay. Additionally, the weather was beginning to turn and Akeem had often taken seasonal jobs in the suburbs doing landscaping and carpentry. At this point it was reasonable to assume he had been picked up by a day labor crew and was bedding down in the suburbs until the job was complete. However, when he didn't return that first weekend, people started to worry. Not even Porsha could explain his absence.

When I arrived at Frank's on the second Monday of Akeem's disappearance, people were eager to try and track him down. But with no fixed address and limited access to a regular cell phone number, tracking down a missing homeless person is nearly impossible. I started making phone calls to a few shelters and soup kitchens in the surrounding areas but to no avail. Over the next several days, I called police stations, jails, and prisons, but no one had any information. For the next two weeks, everyone remained dumbfounded. Finally, I had the idea of trying to find his original intake form in the stacks of paperwork that flooded my office filing cabinets. There were well over 1,200 registered clients and the intake forms were sorted by date. So, if I could figure out the approximate year Akeem filled out his intake form, then it might be possible to locate an emergency contact number or previous address.

After rummaging through forms all morning, I finally found the name "Akeem" along with a corresponding date of birth and consequently discovered a major flaw in the initial search: Akeem was his Muslim name. His legal name was Jonathan Morris. I immediately called Camden County jail and they confirmed that he had been in custody for three weeks for failure to pay child support. He was approximately $9,000 behind on payments. If he had the funds to pay what he owed, he could have left that afternoon. But with no financial resources he had to remain locked up until he saw a judge. Two weeks later he stood before a judge who declared him indigent and ordered his release. Legally, this didn't erase the debt and Akeem was still expected to make future payments, but since he had no means for compliance, chances were good that somewhere down the line he would have to go through this process all over again. Essentially, Akeem's number would pop up in a stack of warrants sometime next year, police would throw him in jail again, taxpayers would pay for a few weeks of accommodations, guards would endure overpopulation, and a judge's time would continue to be wasted adjudicating a case that was going nowhere.

Unfortunately, this type of unproductive judicial cycle happens to many homeless offenders. While a person cannot be thrown in jail for debt, a person can be thrown in jail for failure to obey a court order. This includes orders to pay child support or other fines for things such as an open container or loitering. For people with financial means, a judge can order that the fines be garnished through a person's wages, savings, and/or tax refund. This solution almost guarantees that the person will never be arrested again for this offense since payments are being made directly through a paycheck or banking institution. However, for a homeless person who has no wages to garnish, a judge simply declares the person indigent *for the time being*. If fines remain unpaid, a warrant can be reissued at a later date. Unless that person has secured a way for paying the fine, then the catch-and-release cycle continues indefinitely. Understandably, people should pay their fines and financially take care of their children. Akeem was in the wrong and should have been held accountable. But there has to be a better solution for achieving compliance rather than wasting resources by endlessly throwing people into jail who have no money.

Volunteerism and Good Intentions

During Mission Year, I lived in a house of six people, but there were five other Mission Year houses spread between Camden and Philadelphia. At least once a week, the 40 or so Mission Year members would get together at the Mission Year office on the corner of 10th and Spring Garden for "City Wide." City Wide consisted of formal and informal trainings where people shared stories, ate food, and embraced fellowship. Every now and again, a speaker would stop by to teach on a variety of issues including poverty, local history, racism, gentrification, sustainability, and community. A few City Wide events involved field trips and overnights. About two months into the year in early October, we engaged in an overnight training called Urban Solitude. Urban Solitude was a 24-hour training that encouraged us to explore Philadelphia, meet lots of people, and navigate the city without conventional means. The guidelines for Urban Solitude were as follows: You could only bring a sleeping bag and one bus ticket for the ride home. You weren't allowed to bring money, a phone, or any form of entertainment. While outsiders might dismiss Urban Solitude as some weird elitist exercise in poverty tourism, it was far from it. Participants were well aware that we weren't poor, had resources if needed, and were only doing this for 24 hours. The purpose of Urban Solitude wasn't to see what it was like to "live on the streets." That would be an absurd and borderline offensive objective. Instead, the purpose was to get to know the city, its people, and its resources beyond conventional methods.

Obviously, one of the biggest concerns was finding something to eat and the quickest way to find out the location of free food was to talk to people who were homeless. The homeless knew the location of every soup kitchen, the schedule of every charity that stopped by the parks, and a few tricks for tracking restaurants that threw out copious amounts of unsold food. When it came to restaurants, this wasn't garbage bags full of leftovers. This was fresh food that was being thrown out in the same grocery bag it had arrived in. A homeless man named LeRoy, who I met at the subway stop of JFK Plaza (with the famous "LOVE" statue) told me that, "You'll never go hungry living in Philadelphia." On LeRoy's advice, I opted for lunch at a soup kitchen and dinner was provided by a church group at Logan Square. Not only did these meals provide the opportunity for meeting more people and learning about homelessness in the city, they also gave me a way to connect with other volunteers and agencies who were committed to the issue. This type of networking would prove useful later on.

At first, LeRoy's claim of food abundance seemed exaggerated, but his sentiment was reinforced a few weeks later when I met a guy at a food trailer outside a Catholic church near 13th and Market. I'm not Catholic, but every now and again I liked to step inside an old church and take in the architecture and atmosphere. This particular church occasionally held brief noonday services throughout the week. Upon exiting the service, I stopped by my favorite food trailer guy to buy a cheesesteak. There's a big debate in Philly between "Pat's" and "Geno's" cheesesteaks on South 9th Street. In my opinion, they're both overrated and overpriced. I prefer my cheesesteaks off a food cart.

As I waited in line, I noticed a guy sitting up against a wall surrounded by his belongings. I asked him if he wanted anything, and he replied, "A hot dog with ketchup." Mark and I sat on the sidewalk and ate lunch together for about 30 minutes. When the meal was over, I offered to buy him a hot dog for the road, but he declined. Mark didn't appear to be in any position to turn down free food, but his rationale was that he didn't want to eat so much that he would have to use the restroom. He went on to mention that while food was relatively accessible in Philadelphia, public accommodations were not. Therefore, Mark had devised a schedule. He knew when and where he could eat as well as when and where he could use the restroom. It was one of those small details that most people don't think twice about, but when a person's life is dictated by public charity, adhering to someone else's schedule is necessary. In Mark's case, he ate dinner at a nearby soup kitchen that didn't open until 6:00 p.m. He didn't want to eat too much now and risk getting ahead of schedule.

Beyond food security, there are countless other issues that volunteers, charities, and advocates attempt to address every day in Philadelphia and Camden: job training, mental health, affordable housing, education, energy cost, crime, addiction, and adequate emergency shelter. The needs in Camden are so arduous that they even caught the attention of ABC's *20/20* and *Extreme Makeover: Home Edition*, and in 2007 both of these programs shined a national spotlight on Camden's abject poverty through a couple of hour-long television specials. Diane Sawyer and the *20/20* crew arrived first and highlighted the lives of several families through the perspectives of their children. All of the families interviewed were living in poverty, at least one family was functionally homeless, and there were varying degrees of drug abuse, criminality, and domestic violence showcased throughout the hour. The national interest in that *20/20* special was so intense that ABC decided to do a follow-up with Ty Pennington and *Extreme Makeover: Home Edition.*

Extreme Makeover: Home Edition descended into Camden in mid-summer 2007 and chose to build a new home for one of the families featured in the *20/20* special. Coincidentally, the family chosen was connected with the afterschool program Urban Promise, which I also volunteered with in addition to working at the homeless shelter. The location of the new home was located next door to Urban Promise's main office building and, as a volunteer with Urban Promise, I was allowed to help with the project. Out of sheer curiosity, I visited the set and walked through the construction site a few times after dark when no one was around, but I declined to work on the project. My main problem with the whole fiasco was that *Extreme Makeover: Home Edition* was choosing to build a million-dollar home in the middle of the 'hood. On television, the camera only supplied close-ups of the beautiful new home with its pristine yard, open floor plan, and picturesque windows. However, anyone who takes five minutes to walk around the neighborhood realizes that the home is completely out-of-place and would eventually cause abrupt economic turmoil for the receiving family as well as their neighbors. Within months of Ty Pennington leaving, this is exactly what happened. While the house was paid in full, the receiving family soon found themselves stuck with enormous tax and energy bills. These are the bills that people have to pay forever. Unable to afford the home's upkeep, the family moved out within three years only to find themselves in even more economic and social chaos. This time ABC wasn't there to help.

Now that Camden was the national tragedy *du jour*, donations came pouring into various nonprofit agencies throughout the city. While Frank's did see a modest increase in monetary donations, most donations sent to the shelter were unnecessary or completely useless household goods. Some of the items included used toasters, swimsuits, yoga mats, encyclopedias, and bath toys. Keep in mind, these weren't random items dropped off by local people from the suburbs in a flippant manner that many of us might drop off an amalgamation of items at

Goodwill. These were boxes of items shipped by the United States Postal Service from people around the country who had seen Camden's poverty via *20/20*. Therefore, someone deliberately shipped swimsuits and encyclopedias to a homeless shelter. Although well-intended, the shelter only had so much storage space and it was imperative that the space was used for essential goods and services. Useless items only added to the constant stress and frustration. For my boss, Ms. Sharron, the last straw was a set of four large boxes shipped from California. She opened the boxes to show me that each box had been filled with stuffed animal keychains. There was also a hopeful note attached mentioning that the stuffed animals could be used to lift the spirits of the homeless. She then closed each box and pointed to the $35 shipping charge per box—a total of $140. She had removed a few keychains for the few children running around the shelter and then asked me to throw the boxes away. There just wasn't any room left for this type of nonsense and, frankly, the concept was patronizing. As she left the office, she asked, "Why didn't they just send the money?"

Money and volunteers are the lifeblood of many nonprofit organizations. If a person wants to donate anything other than their time or money, it's best to ask first. Otherwise, filtering through unusable donations just becomes more work for the staff. At Frank's Place, small groups of high school and college students regularly donated their time and would circulate through to help with cooking, cleaning, organizing, and sorting. Most would only stay for a couple of days during a weeklong volunteer trip to the city, but their help and interest were always appreciated. After the *20/20* special, more students were volunteering their time to the point where there wasn't always enough work to go around. It was hard to figure out what to do with 15 college students who were untrained and only dropped by for a day to help. By the time someone taught all 15 people what to do, the day was nearly over.

During these times of volunteer abundance, Ms. Sharron would tell students to "just go be with the people" in the upstairs dining hall or outside patio. The students' initial hesitancy was palpable. They had shown up to perform manual labor and now the staff was handing them decks of cards and board games and telling them to go talk to people. Watching 18-year-olds approach people at the shelter was like watching a first date. Everything about them was awkward and uncertain. Most of them traveled in groups of two or three, hoping a partner would initiate the conversation. It was understandable and I remember these feelings too from my first volunteering experiences. The students were working with a stigmatized population in a stigmatized city and were constantly reminded of their outsider status. They didn't want to do anything that upset current social norms and they knew that they were drawing attention to themselves just by being there. And it probably didn't help that they all wore matching t-shirts commemorating their trip to Camden.

Even though these interactions seem trite in the short-term, these are the interactions that foster long-term relationships and make substantive change possible. When people come in with grand ideas about changing the system overnight, they forget that these communities have existed long before they arrived and will be here long after they are gone. Organizing a food pantry is helpful, but once a group of volunteers leave that pantry is still going to need maintenance. However, if volunteers take time to learn about the people they are serving, then that lays the foundation for genuine relationships and long-term commitment to the issue. Volunteers can't get emotionally connected to sorting food bags, but they can get connected to the people receiving those bags. These personal connections are what keep volunteers coming back.

Frustratingly, this long-term ethic wasn't embraced by every volunteer group that came through Camden and, unfortunately, some volunteers seemingly came into the city for purely voyeuristic reasons—a type of poverty tourism. Camden had a reputation and they wanted to tell everyone that they had seen its exoticism firsthand. This was no more obvious than when a group of 12 white college students flew in from an elite West Coast university for a week upon hearing Diane Sawyer's plea for help. Through a couple of phone calls, they were put in touch with our house. Requests for hospitality and information weren't unusual, but this particular group approached volunteerism like a sightseeing adventure. There were no requests for meeting people or learning about people's situations. They just wanted to visit every location they had heard about on television and read about online. Each person had spent close to $1,000 between airfare, food, and lodging, and, understandably, felt entitled to get his or her money's worth. Alas, the only way to fulfill such a demanding agenda was by running from one location to the next as quickly as possible. This included appropriate requests such as visiting shelters and the Camden Waterfront as well as inappropriate requests such as visiting Tent City and driving by known drug corners documented on *20/20*. While I can appreciate the enthusiasm to learn, I can't just invade people's privacy by marching a group of 12 unknown college students into a homeless encampment or driving by a drug corner like we're on safari. There is a thin line between sincere curiosity and exploitation, and without first establishing relationships, that line is easily crossed.

Relationships and Family

Personal relationships are built on "mutual vulnerability" (Nouwen, 2004, p. 12). If volunteers remain emotionally distant from those they are serving, then the relationship can only remain professional between a person with resources and a person receiving resources. Therefore, if a volunteer wants to learn about the vulnerabilities of a community, then that volunteer must be willing to share his or her own vulnerabilities. Additionally, strong personal relationships have a sense of give and take. In many instances, volunteers want to give and give and give and expect nothing in return. Even though this altruism is admirable, over time this model only solidifies the chasm between those who give and those who receive. The longer this arrangement remains, the easier it is to fall into a relationship built on hierarchy.

When I first began working at Frank's, I too often reinforced this hierarchy. As a college-educated volunteer, I was eager to use my education and talents to support the needs of Camden's homeless community. And, for the most part, I was really good at the professional aspects of my job. I handled intake forms, packed food bags, performed basic maintenance, and helped clean. There were instances when people offered to help, but I was usually dismissive of their requests and instead encouraged them to relax. At the time, I thought I was doing a service by taking on so many jobs. In hindsight, I realize how refusing someone's help can seem paternalistic. This isn't to say that I didn't try to build personal relationships through informal conversations. After all, I was handing out doughnuts and listening to Eagles games at the transportation center. Yet, even this act was focused on what I could do for others instead of focusing on all the talents within the group.

The importance of interdependence finally hit me through two major events. The first event happened in early November when more people began utilizing Frank's to escape the oncoming winter weather. This time of year also brought an end to the harvest season, so more and more agricultural workers were finding themselves unemployed. While many migrant workers headed south for the winter harvest, some remained up north due to family obligations or health reasons. For example, there were several older gentlemen whose bodies could no longer handle the long bus rides or who had ongoing health problems requiring monthly appointments with their family doctors. These individuals would wait out the winter season up north and return to the fields the following spring. This November influx brought in a large portion of Spanish-speaking clientele for whom I was unprepared. The intake forms were lengthy, asked very specific questions, and I didn't speak a word of Spanish, but Riccardo did.

Until this moment, Riccardo was fairly low-key around the shelter. He hobbled into the shelter every morning on a long-ago injured ankle and spent most of the day in an upstairs corner chair reading old newspapers and drinking endless cups of coffee. When my first Spanish-speaking client sat down in my office, I scrambled for help. As stated earlier, Camden had a relatively large Latino population and many residents jumped back-and-forth between speaking English and Spanish. Unfortunately, I was having a hard time finding someone fluent enough to translate the intricate concepts used on the intake form: e.g., social security, disability benefits, Medicaid. Most bilingual people at the shelter were just learned enough to hold a basic conversation across language backgrounds. And a few wise guys just knew the dirty words. But Riccardo's language skills were first-rate. He grew up in an English-speaking household with a hint of Spanglish from his Mexican American grandparents. At seventeen, Riccardo began working all over the United States in agriculture and did so for decades before landing in New Jersey. Thanks to his co-workers, he became fluent in Spanish as well as the many dialects that come from various Latin American countries.

Now Riccardo sat in my office next to the clients and helped us work through the intake forms. Additionally, his informal conversations with the clients helped the staff figure out client needs that weren't specifically marked on the form such as scheduling doctors' appointments or planning travel arrangements. Without Riccardo's help, many of these

Spanish-speaking clients would have simply had their information filed and then they would have retreated upstairs into isolation since they couldn't communicate their needs to anyone else. As time passed and Riccardo's services continued to be utilized more and more, there was also a visible change in his behavior. No longer did Riccardo sit alone with old newspapers in an upstairs corner. Instead, he meandered through the first-floor offices and drank his coffee while waiting on Spanish-speaking clients. When there were no intakes, he helped people in the clothing area and even answered phones. Riccardo's work was valued and gave him a sense of purpose. He was no longer just a client on the receiving end of a social hierarchy; he was a contributing co-worker.

The second major event that forced me to reassess the interdependent nature of relationships dealt with finances. While living in Camden, I didn't have much disposable income, but every now and again I would make small purchases for friends who were homeless: food, bus tickets, clean socks and underwear, and holiday gifts. Again, I never expected anything in return, and besides, who had ever *asked for money* from a homeless person? It is expected that well-to-do people provide resources and homeless people receive resources. Yet, over time these one-sided exchanges only perpetuate a social hierarchy that makes mutual relationships between the housed and the homeless nearly impossible.

This accepted hierarchy was challenged in mid–December when I had to leave work early for a meeting in Philadelphia. The roundtrip bus ticket only cost $2.60, but I had no cash and consequently, had to backtrack home to pick up a bus pass from a roommate. Riff noticed me getting ready to leave and asked what I was doing. Once I told him that I needed to make the 30 minute detour home to grab a bus pass in order to catch a bus that was currently located right across the street, he demanded that I sit back down and continue working. He was going to take care of this. Riff grabbed a paper coffee cup, emptied the modest change in his pockets, and then ran upstairs to the common area. Within five minutes he returned with a cup full of coins, thanks to the contributions of a dozen or so homeless people. In total, it was a little more than $8. I suggested that the extra money be returned, but everyone insisted that I use it to buy dinner in Philly: a cheesesteak and soda only cost $5 off a food trailer.

As the year went on, these types of interactions became routine. No longer were people from the shelter just homeless clientele in need of resources and support. Instead, resources and support circulated in both directions and a group of us had become like family. We had parties that celebrated birthdays, baby showers, and graduations. We attended countywide fundraisers together, complete with formal attire and dancing shoes. We offered emotional support for one another during tough times like hospitalizations and funerals. We argued over everything from sports to religion and politics. And a group of us even took a family vacation together to Atlantic City.

By far, the Atlantic City trip was the best family experience. Since most of the people who worked at Frank's did so on a voluntary basis, Ms. Sharron convinced the board to scrape together a little extra money to send all the workers down to Atlantic City for a three-day weekend in late June. It was a two-hour train ride to the coast and, once we got there, the 15 of us had to squeeze into just two hotel rooms. Each room was a two-bedroom suite with a full kitchenette, but either way, plenty of people were going to end up sleeping on the floor. One suite was for Ms. Sharron, her three children, and two grandchildren. For three straight days, Ms. Sharron just stayed in her room and cooked. She kept the door propped open so at any time someone could just walk in her room and eat pancakes, bacon, fried chicken, greens, potato salad, fried okra, or a whole host of other delicious items. There was also plenty of sweet tea on tap.

The other nine of us stayed in the second suite: three college students and six homeless people. To keep us entertained, Ms. Sharron gave us each a $20 stipend for the weekend. Since we were in Atlantic City, I figured that someone was going to lose all of his or her money in the first hour gambling. But no one did. One guy bought bait and a six-pack and fished off the pier every day. A few others just bought beer and watched television in the hotel room. I tried to convince them to explore the shore, but they just laughed at my naïve request. For a homeless person, what's a better vacation than a nice room and cable? The last of us went down to the beach, climbed on the rocks, and swam in the ocean; without swim trunks, Akeem just ran around in boxer briefs. And by the end of the weekend, the majority of my $20 went to boardwalk funnel cakes and kettle corn. At the end of each day, our room cooked up some popcorn and flipped on a movie. There were no real sleeping arrangements, but if you wanted one of the two or three spots available per bed, you had to crawl in early.

The Cycle

On Tuesday morning, a regular named Martin walked into the main floor office space. Martin was loud, colorful, and openly gay. He also battled a vicious crack addiction and the scars from his battle were everywhere. Most visible was his ashy skin from dehydration and the burn marks that encircled his lips from using inadequate paraphernalia. Less visible was the Hepatitis C and emotional damage that came from the rampant prostitution he engaged in to support his habit. He was only 28 years old, but his body wore much older and he was clearly tired of the life he had been living. When he entered the room, he threw his hands up and said, "Hey everyone, I finally got clean!" Ms. Sharron just put her hands on her hips and looked at him quizzically. "Oh, just hush! Since when did you get clean?" Martin replied, "Well, I haven't smoked crack today." It was only 9:30 a.m.

We all got a good laugh out of Martin's antics and attempts at humor, but there was also a deep sadness to his very real struggle. After all, like many addicts, this wasn't the first time Martin had declared his sobriety. On at least two occasions, he was even shipped up to Newark for a treatment program. The problem was that once treatment was over, he came right back to Camden. Drug counselors often encourage addicts to avoid everything from their life of addiction, including friends who are addicts and locations where their vices are easily accessible. However, for addicts in Camden, there is nowhere within city limits where people can escape the temptation of drugs. And having lived his entire life in Camden, where else was Martin supposed to go? Martin was caught in his own ruthless cycle, unable to find a permanent escape route. Unfortunately, the cycle of poverty, homelessness, and addiction in Camden extended far beyond individuals. Even though we celebrated the success of one person entering treatment, obtaining a job, or securing housing, it was inevitable that 2–3 new clients were coming through the door every day. By the end of the week, Martin had disappeared back into the thralls of the streets. It wasn't unexpected and we knew he'd be back in a couple of weeks trying to get clean again.

Short of locking him in a room for weeks on end, there's only so much a person can do for a drug addict who hasn't yet hit bottom.

It was now early July and I only had a month left in Mission Year. There were no afterschool programs going on in the summer, so I found myself spending more and more time at Frank's even though this was a slower time of year and there was less work to do. During the warm summer months, most people preferred to stay outside and only stopped by the shelter for a quick meal at lunchtime. Within 30 minutes of lunch service, the shelter was mostly empty. It was also slow because people had recently gotten their checks on the first of the month. With checks in hand, people found food and shelter through other means. Some of the homeless ended up renting a room for a week or two so they could enjoy the privacy not afforded to them by a shelter. People who had homes, but insufficient food, could finally buy groceries and avoid the sometimes monotonous food options that the shelter offered. And, of course, there were some who cashed their checks and got high. Whether the government checks went to housing, food, or drugs, by about the 20th of each month, everyone would run out money and the shelter would slowly start to fill again. Within a week and a half, this cycle would start right up again just like clockwork.

On that first Friday in July after Martin had disappeared, things were slow and I was just looking to pass the time. During lunch I wandered outside and enjoyed a couple of fruit cups in a folding chair propped against the black iron gate that stretched the front of the building. A stranger approached and started giving a sob story in an attempt to squeeze a few bucks out of me. Before he could even formally ask for the money, Pitbull rushed up from behind and started yelling, "Titus! Leave Josh alone. He works here, man." Pit was 5'5" and weighed at least 250 pounds. His nickname fit both his size and outward persona, but underneath his gruff exterior was a big softy who wandered around the shelter all day listening to Prince's *Purple Rain* over and over again on an old Walkman. However, at this moment, Pit was genuinely irate because there was an unwritten rule about begging the staff for money. As soon as Titus realized his mistake, he apologized and instead just tried to bum a cigarette. I didn't smoke, but Pit had a small amount of loose tobacco and some rolling papers. The two of them continued loitering on the sidewalk while I returned to my office to finish the last bit of paperwork before the weekend.

40

When I got back to my office, a rather attractive 19-year-old girl was waiting at my desk and she was dressed for summer: white tank top, Daisy Duke cut offs, tan skin, and long brunette hair. It wouldn't have been the outfit I'd have recommended for a cute white girl walking around downtown Camden, but, then again, I had seen more provocative choices. Despite the confidence she placed in her revealing wardrobe, she carried herself like many of the wide-eyed lost volunteers that strolled through Frank's on a weekly basis. She was shy and out-of-place. While most volunteers served in groups, it wasn't unusual for a group leader to stop by a few days early and meet with the staff in order to figure out how to prepare the rest of the team members. "Can I help you?" "Yeah," she replied, "Gerald sent me in here and told me to wait for Josh." Assuming she was a group leader with a local church or school, I began asking her about how many people were in her group and what days they wanted to serve. She looked confused. "It's just me and I need some clothes and some lunch if they're still serving."

Her name was Nicole and she had just graduated from high school. She grew up only 10 minutes away in a nice New Jersey suburb and, like every other suburban teenager, was set to go to college in the fall. But she had a meth problem. It started as a social habit during her junior year. She said she only used small amounts every couple of weeks at house parties and after school events like football games and dances. However, once graduation was over and her friends slowly left town, she started using on her own. There were no more parties to "look forward to" to sustain her habit. Now she got high on her own schedule. Her parents knew she was struggling with the transition from high school to college, but they didn't know she was using. To help, they offered to let her live at home during her freshman year and enroll her in a few community college classes. Sadly, she declined and hopped on a bus to Camden.

For 30 minutes I begged her to leave town. I tried getting her to call her parents, but she didn't want them to know where she was. So, I just told her to get back on the bus and go home. I even offered to take the ride with her. Nicole was green out here and had no idea what she was getting herself into. There was still time for her to turn back before she stumbled down these dark corridors. Once she spent a night on these streets, there was no turning back. After that, the only way she would get out of here was by going through it. But she calmly refused

41

my appeals and just continued to ask for clothing and food. I walked her to the clothing area and retreated upstairs to pack her a meal. Lunch had been over for more than an hour, but there were always plenty of sandwiches, fruits, and snacks in the kitchen.

A month later I was working my final week at Frank's. Thursday, August 9th, was my last day, and on Friday I would take a train to the Philadelphia International Airport with everything I owned. During that week, I was intent on arriving early each day and staying late. I wanted to contribute as much help as possible as well as savor those final moments with fellow staff members and clients. The main doors didn't open until 8:00 a.m., so when I arrived at 7:30, I had to walk around back to the rear entrance. The rear entrance was nestled at the end of a driveway and surrounded by overgrown foliage. Weeds and vines found consolation as they weaved in and out of the adjacent six-foot-tall chain-link fence. There were also a few old benches back there where staff sat and took cigarette breaks throughout the day. Walking up the driveway, I noticed someone sleeping on a bench. Although the gates were locked at night, people sometimes hopped the fence in an attempt to sleep with an added sense of security.

The person sleeping on the bench was wrapped in multiple layers of oversized sweatshirts and a raggedy hood obstructed her face. I walked over to shake her awake. She mumbled in protest, but the shelter was opening and it was time to move. She sat up, pulled back her hood, and combed her hair. It was Nicole. It had only been a month, but she was nearly unrecognizable. Her hair was stringy and unwashed, and by the look of her face she had lost almost 20 pounds. Nicole's complexion, once glowing tan, was now chalky and specked with small cuts, scabs, and a few cigarette burns. She was too strung out to bother with any questions or concerns, but the evidence was obvious. Nicole had been binging hard and supporting her habit through prostitution. At that point, all I could do was steer her towards the front gate where a small group of homeless people were waiting for Frank's to open and start serving breakfast.

Seeing Nicole's condition right before leaving Camden was heart-breaking, but it also provided perspective. The reality was that life moved on and, unfortunately, new people were coming into the fold of homelessness every day. While we should celebrate sobriety, job security, and housing independence, we should also recognize that for every

42

happy ending, someone else's nightmare is just beginning. The cycle never ends, and that's why a steady and realistic approach is essential. Overzealous approaches just lead to burnout and nihilism. By the end of Mission Year, I had seen tragedies and witnessed miracles. And I had learned not to place too much emphasis on either. Homelessness had existed in Camden long before I got there and it was going to be there long after I left. My job was to simply do what I could, with what I had, in the time available.

When I finished my undergraduate degree in May 2006, the original plan was to only defer graduate school for a year. However, by the summer of 2007, I was seriously considering staying in Camden and forgoing graduate school altogether. I loved the work, I loved the people, and I loved the city. If I wanted to continue working on the issue of homelessness, this was ground zero and I didn't see any benefit in returning to a classroom in the middle of Michigan. There was some concern about finding a job in Camden to support myself, but I had cobbled together a few part-time leads along with some communal housing options that would have made staying possible. Coincidentally, one of the part-time leads was through Frank's Place. Knowing that Will and I were leaving, Ms. Sharron approached the board earlier that spring and asked them to fund a part-time position. The two of us probably completed 40 hours of paperwork per week between handling new client intakes and logging daily services. They were going to need someone to fill that role. The part-time gig was only 20 hours per week at minimum wage, but it was a start.

In June, I approached Ms. Sharron about the position. I already knew the entire administrative system and Ms. Sharron loved me, so I figured she'd be thrilled that I was even considering the opportunity. Sitting in her office, she just scowled at my request. "Listen, Blondie, if you don't go back to school I'm going to whoop you!" I was a bit confused by this response, but the lecture that followed helped clear things up. In short, Ms. Sharron loved me and was sad to see me go, but I had an educational opportunity that so many people at Frank's would have given anything for. Every day, people who are homeless struggle to earn a G.E.D., a vocational certificate, or a college degree so they can hopefully find employment and live with some semblance of stability. For me not to capitalize on an educational opportunity that was right in front of me would have been an insult. Besides, Frank's wasn't going anywhere. Ms. Sharron assured me that I could always come back and work once I had finished graduate school. But in the long run, I could be far more useful with the letters "Ph.D." after my name and the credibility that comes with that. I knew what I had seen firsthand in Camden. Now it was prudent to step away and study these types of cultural complexities a bit more dispassionately. So for the next six years, I went to school. What follows is the culmination of that initial research on homelessness.

PART II
RESEARCHING HOMELESSNESS

3. Defining Homelessness

Contextualizing the parameters of homelessness is a difficult task from the start because there is no agreed-upon understanding as to what constitutes homelessness. In 1987, the McKinney Homeless Act attempted to define the homeless as "an individual who lacks a fixed, regular, and adequate nighttime residence" (Lang, 2007, p. 47). However, the inadequacies of this definition are highlighted in its multiple interpretations. For example, this definition could include: a person with no shelter living on the street; a person living in a shelter; a person living in temporary or transitional housing; or a person living with family or friends. An early study on homelessness found that 9 percent of the U.S. American population fit this government-imposed definition of homelessness based on the McKinney Homeless Act; however, when people were asked to self-report their housing situation, 15 percent indicated that they had been homeless at some point in the previous year (Lang, 2007). These discrepancies between government estimates and individual accounts are noteworthy and should be taken into consideration when attempting to accurately define the homeless population.

In an effort to more accurately quantify the homeless population, several coalitions for the homeless have attempted new methodologies that track services rendered by shelters, soup kitchens, and various government programs. In 2011, the National Alliance to End Homelessness reported that an average of 643,067 people were homeless at any given time over the course of one year. Additionally, in 2004, the National Law Center on Homelessness estimated that 3.5 million people experienced homelessness during a given year. In regard to these numbers, the National Coalition for the Homeless (2009) mentions that not all people who are homeless use services and therefore, the numbers are most likely higher than these estimates. Reporting on some of the statistical breakdowns, 26 percent of the homeless have a mental illness, 13 percent have a disability, the average shelter stay is between 51–70 days (National Coalition, 2009), and 40 percent of the homeless are without a shelter on any given night (National Alliance, 2011).

While these "official" numbers are impressive, some scholars suggest that we proceed with caution. For instance, in his essay "The Problem of Homelessness Is Exaggerated," Rosen (2007) asserts that there are no accurate data to quantify the homeless population because those who avoid the homeless have no interest in counting them and those who help the homeless often exaggerate their numbers in order to receive increased government funding. In the end, the homeless are positioned according to their monetary worth by both those who are apathetic as well as those whose paychecks and positions depend on providing services.

As callous as his analysis may sound, Rosen does provide an important critical lens that leads to one striking question about the issue of homelessness: if these agencies are collecting money in order to end homelessness, are their programs working? Observantly, it seems that agencies working to end homelessness would be working against their monetary interest if in fact they were successful in ending homelessness. Essentially, a decreasing homeless population would lead to less government funding and less personnel. While I do not presume that people intentionally sabotage the system for the personal benefit of receiving increased government grants, much of the data collected over the past 50 years does support the idea that little progress has been made at ending poverty and homelessness despite the massive government subsidies that are continually poured into these systems.

In analyzing the failed systems of government programs aimed at helping the poor, some scholars point to the complicated bureaucracies that eat away most of the funding before monies reach those individuals for whom they were intended. For example, in 1992, $190 billion was spent on poverty programs in the United States, but "much of that $190 billion [was] not 'for persons of limited income' at all, but for the poverty industry—bureaucrats, caseworkers, service providers, and a grab-bag of vendors in the private sector who plan, implement, and evaluate social programs on government contracts" (Murray, 1992, p. xiii).

By 2011, welfare spending for people with low income had increased

32 percent within the previous four years (Congressional Research Service, 2012; Ginsberg, 2012) and the federal government was spending approximately $1.03 trillion on welfare programs making "welfare that year the government's largest expenditure" (May 2012, para. 1; Congressional Research Service, 2012). When looking at the programs where money has been invested to specifically address the homeless population, take for example The Homeless Prevention and Rapid Re-Housing Program. In 2009, this program invested $1.5 *billion* to assist about 700,000 homeless people (National Alliance, 2011). Despite these massive economic efforts, the homeless population remained virtually unchanged from 2009–2011. In a poignant summary about government programs aimed at helping the poor, Blackwell (2012) notes that "The massive transfers of wealth of the Lyndon B. Johnson era were sputtering out, having achieved little. And some people said then: 'We declared war on poverty, and poverty won'" (para. 3).

Intercultural Communication

Part of the reason little progress has been made when it comes to ending homelessness may have to do with the fact that economic segregation has drastically increased over the years and that the upper class continues to make policy and financial decisions for the lower class despite having little to no contact with a lower-class reality (Murray, 2012). Coupled with class segregation is also the availability and access to voice in public space in order to steer dialogue about socio-economic policy. Commenting on voice, hooks (2000) writes, "We live in a society where the poor have no public voice" (p. 5). Therefore, when it comes to crafting policies that impact the poor and homeless, a system has been created where the reputed beneficiaries are locked out of conversations that have direct bearing on their livelihoods.

This growing distance between class statuses is why this research argues that homelessness is uniquely positioned to be discussed within the parameters of intercultural communication. Notably, this argument is in line with the work of Daniel (1970), Whiting (1971), and Philipsen (1976) who each highlighted class status as a variable in intercultural communication research. In regard to homelessness, navigating intercultural boundaries is a process where people who are homeless and people who are housed continuously negotiate class identity, government welfare, and public policies. Due to these constant negotiations, it would be advantageous if these groups of people could better understand each other's cultural perspectives.

At its genesis, the field of intercultural communication was formed in the 1940s when Edward Hall's work was used to educate U.S. American diplomats through the U.S. Department of State's Foreign Service Institute (Leeds-Hurwitz, 1990; Moon, 1996, 2010). Prior to the introduction of Hall's work, there was a growing frustration that U.S. American diplomats did not fully understand the language or the culture of the countries where they were being stationed and many U.S. American diplomats simply wanted to know how to better interact with people in the various host countries (Leeds-Hurwitz, 1990). In addition, the U.S. American government stood to benefit from diplomats becoming more interculturally effective with regard to international and business affairs (Leeds-Hurwitz, 1990; Moon, 1996). To this end, much of Hall's work pulled from the academic fields of anthropology and linguistics to establish a model that advocated for a broader education about the histories, customs, politics, and economic policies of the countries where U.S. diplomats would be serving.

Hall's emphasis on the interactions between cultures began the "shift from viewing cultures one at a time to studying interactions between members of different cultures..." (Leeds-Hurwitz, 1990, p. 263). While this shift began as a practical response for training U.S. American diplomats for intercultural interactions abroad, the field of intercultural communication burgeoned in the academy during the 1960s and 1970s when professors and students began researching intercultural interactions more intensely (Leeds-Hurwitz, 1990; Moon, 1996). As a field closely connected to anthropology, one of the first goals of intercultural communication was to describe intercultural interactions (González, 2010; Leeds-Hurwitz, 1990; Mendoza, 2005). Through these descriptive analyses, intercultural scholars began to recognize that culture was not static, but rather a more fluid concept that was always changing and evolving through cultural interactions (Martin & Nakayama, 1999).

In addition to thinking about the changing aspects of culture, scholars also began thinking about how to define "culture." Traditionally, the concept of "culture" had been used in reference to international nation-state borders. However, during the 1970s, scholars began "conceptualizing 'culture' in terms of race, social class, and gender identity" (Moon, 1996, p. 72). This work began to highlight the cultural diversity within nation-states (specifically, the diversity within U.S. American culture) and eventually led to the critical turn in the late 1980s/early 1990s when culture began to be conceptualized as a "struggle." Previous to the critical turn, intercultural communication research was housed in the quantitative and interpretive paradigms, which offered different conceptualizations of culture where "researchers address 'micro' contexts" (Martin & Nakayama, 1999, p. 7). For example, "micro context" could address the interpersonal communication strategies between two members of the same community. However, the critical turn articulated that culture was a site of struggle and decidedly referenced how macro systems of power construct intercultural interactions and identities, shape reality, privilege some groups, and marginalize others (Halualani & Nakayama, 2010; Moon, 1996).

While understanding culture as a nation-state had traditionally been defined as a concrete idea that was singular and embraced by all members of a particular nation-state, these new ideas framed culture as a site where multiple interpretations of reality can and do exist based on a person's position within a culture. As articulated by Moon (2010):

> The move from viewing culture as unproblematically shared and relatively stable to one that acknowledges culture as a contested zone and thus in flux opens up new possibilities for intercultural scholars, allowing us to understand that rather than being comprised of "a reality," culture is a space of competing realities embedded in power relations with all but the dominant or hegemonic version getting short shrift [p. 38].

Ultimately, some scholars suggest that the role of an intercultural scholar who identifies with the critical paradigm is to recognize these power differences and to analyze issues of power within and between cultures (DeTurk, 2001; Halualani & Nakayama, 2010). In total, the enduring trend of intercultural communication has led to a moment where issues of power have become a large part of the growing conversation. Given the clear socio-economic power dynamics involved with the issue of homelessness, it can be argued that while homelessness has largely been absent from the intercultural communication discussion, it is well-suited to be explored within the field.

One way of doing critical intercultural research in relation to homelessness would be to look at issues of power as they exist within the United States between people with different income levels and various housing statuses. In attempting to understand homelessness in the United States, a middle-income U.S. American may have very different ideas about homelessness when compared to a homeless U.S. American because socio-economic difference can create different perspectives. While a recognition of these differences is a good place to begin intercultural conversations about culture, Mendoza (2005) argues that marginalized groups still have to fight for recognition because mainstream understandings about culture are more likely to come from those in positions of power who have the ability to shape and influence culture. As a result, a middle-income U.S. American with a roof over his head is provided a larger platform for addressing the experiences of the homeless while people who are actually homeless are rendered silent even though the homeless could speak more accurately from firsthand experiences.

In order to create more spaces for marginalized voices within the field, some critical intercultural scholars have worked "to redefine what counts as intercultural communication research" (González, 2010, p. 55). By challenging the traditional ideas about research and knowledge production, intercultural communication scholars can expand the field to include "insights and perspectives usually ignored or marginalized" (Moon, 1996, p. 77). Looking back to an early critical intercultural outlook, Whiting (1971) asks scholars to be aware of the class bias that can happen when financially stable researchers study those individuals who are not financially stable. Answering these calls for more inclusive scholarship and researcher self-awareness, a narrative approach to studying homelessness would offer a platform where people who are homeless could discuss their experiences within a scholarly setting. Thus providing valuable insights into the complex culture of homelessness.

Within these contemporary understandings of intercultural communication, homelessness would best be located within two intercultural communication paradigmatic approaches. First, using an interpretive approach, the culture of homelessness can be situated as a subjective experience where "[c]ulture ... is generally seen as socially constructed and emergent..." (Martin & Nakayama, 1999, p. 6). Therefore, not only are the circumstances of becoming a homeless person developed through an ongoing communicative process, but also, one of the ideal ways that a researcher can learn about that process is through an ethnographic study where people who are homeless are given the opportunity to share their lives and narrate their stories. This can happen more vibrantly through qualitative methods. These acts of narration can help better connect scholars who are attempting to end homelessness, with the homeless whose lives depend on the implementation of good social and economic policy. As noted by Martin and Nakayama (1999):

> there is a recognition that intercultural communication research should be more relevant to everyday lives, that theorizing and research should be firmly based in experience, and in turn, should not only be relevant to, but should facilitate, the success of everyday intercultural encounters... [pp. 7–8].

Being homeless can be a very personal struggle and the interpretive approach provides an avenue for uncovering these very personal stories in micro contexts. In the end, mutual understandings between the housed culture and the homeless culture are essential if those who are crafting policies that address homelessness wish to do so in ways that are sensitive and helpful to the homeless community. Embracing narration through the interpretive approach can help foster a better understanding of these cultural differences.

The second paradigmatic approach that could be used to more fully understand the issue of homelessness is the critical humanist approach. Similar to the interpretive approach, the critical humanist approach "assume[s] that reality is socially constructed" (Martin & Nakayama, 1999, p. 8). However, unlike the interpretive approach, the critical humanist approach is more concerned with looking at macro systems of ideology that create power structures, where culture becomes "a site of struggle where various communication meanings are contested" (Martin & Nakayama, 1999, p. 8). Therefore, analyzing homelessness through a critical lens will provide the opportunity of better understanding the systemic elements that create the conditions for homelessness to exist in the first place. Further studying these elements would also allow researchers to better understand why current methods for ending homelessness are not working. Ultimately, the interpretive and critical humanist paradigms can work together to give researchers a more complete understanding of homelessness. Whereas the interpretive approach attempts to highlight the personal accounts of homeless people through personal narratives, the critical humanist approach highlights the larger cultural institutions that create and maintain homelessness.

A Distinct Culture

After positioning homelessness as a phenomenon to be studied through intercultural communication paradigmatic lenses, it is then necessary to assess the distinct cultural markers of the homeless community by documenting common practices regarding lifestyles, customs, priorities, and vernacular. In part, these similarities are driven by shared socio-economic and housing statuses that are vastly different from the experiences of most U.S. Americans. The argument that "social divisions cause cultural differences between socio-economic classes" is not a new academic revelation: it was first observed over 125 years ago. One of the earliest academic accounts of class differences in the United States was Riis' 1890 book, *How the Other Half Lives*. Riis' (1890) original intent was to go to the poor in order to learn about their situation in an effort to start a larger conversation as to how two drastically different worlds of poverty and wealth could coexist in New York City. Upon observing the stark cultural differences between the financially stable and those who lived with dire financial needs, Riis (1890) concluded that most people in positions of power are blind to the realities of those who live in a constant state of poverty and homelessness.

This type of ethnographic work continued throughout the twentieth century with discouragingly similar conclusions. For example, Conover (1984) spent months living among the homeless in the early 1980s and would eventually record his observations in the book, *Rolling Nowhere: Riding the Rails with America's Hoboes*. After living with the homeless and sharing life with the homeless for an extended time period, Conover (1984) concluded his work by stating, "most of us still see hoboes as a race apart, strangers whom we have no need to know and no way of knowing" (p. 281). In this statement, Conover unearths two major observations consistent with Riis. First, people who are homeless are situated and treated as people from a different culture. Second, most housed people avoid the homeless because the homeless offer no measurable value to their lives.

52

At the most fundamental level, avoiding the homeless becomes problematic as it perpetuates a class divide that further distances well-to-do policymakers from the intended beneficiaries of welfare programs. The problems that arrive through this lack of interaction are best described in Campbell and Reeves' (1989) article, "Covering the Homeless: The Joyce Brown Story." In short, Joyce Brown was a homeless woman who continued living her life on the street despite the humanitarian efforts of politicians and doctors to relocate homeless people into transitional housing. In covering this story about homelessness, the initial news media elicited the professional opinions of government officials as well as psychologists, but were negligent in providing any platform where Brown's voice could articulate her wants, needs, and priorities. Finally, 60 Minutes interviewed Joyce Brown and discovered intimate details about her life that were previously void from public discussions on homelessness. Not surprisingly, Brown told a very different story about her life, her needs, and her goals than the politicians and doctors who were given the task of "helping the homeless" through government funding and mental health treatment. The concluding message of Campbell and Reeves' (1989) research is that we must be critical in how we interact with one another across class lines as well as mindful as to how we communicate other people's stories. Try as they might, well-intended welfare efforts will continue to fail when targeted beneficiaries reject program compliance because they believe that certain programs more adequately address the priorities of the policymakers instead of addressing the priorities of the beneficiaries. Addressing homelessness must happen within a dialogical framework, especially when many of those who have the power to make these financial, housing, and health decisions have never experienced the type of social silencing and social policing that oftentimes accompanies homelessness.

In conjunction with public voice, Brown's story is also indicative of larger issues of power and control. As the homeless move through public spaces, their bodies, actions, and behaviors are carefully monitored by larger social pressures aimed at controlling their unwanted status. Not only does the housed population find ways to speak for the homeless, but the housed population insists that the "homeless *need* to be contained, enclosed, disciplined, or excluded" (Feldman, 2004, p. 5). For example, in 2012 the city of Denver passed an "urban camping" ban in an effort to coax homeless people off city streets ("Homeless

Camping," 2012). While those who supported the bill claimed they did so in an effort to protect the homeless by persuading them into city shelters, opponents of the bill noted "that even if the city doubled its current shelter capacity, it would still not reach the necessary number of people who are in need" ("Homeless Camping," 2012, para. 6). In the end, the only way most homeless people could remain in compliance with the new ordinance was by leaving Denver.

This type of controlling behavior is indicative of putting someone in his proverbial place in order to mold more socially appropriate behaviors. This distinction of "appropriate behaviors" between the housed and the homeless also exacerbates the cultural differences between these two groups. As outlined by DePastino (2003), the homeless are not valued in mainstream society because the homeless represent the very antithesis of what it means to have a place in the world. This place is rooted in the idea of "home." The foundational idea of "home" communicates one's place as a contributing member of society (DePastino, 2003). Without a home, a person is viewed as an outsider with no roots, no direction, and no value, thus furthering the class divide. Moreover, home is a central location for family, work, and community. Therefore, the absence of home leaves a person on the margins of the dominant social fabric and he is positioned as having nothing of value to contribute. In the end, society constrains the behaviors of the homeless by communicating its collective distaste for the homeless. The desired outcome of these collective actions would be to shame the homeless into making decisions that will allow them to more actively contribute to the larger community, through traditional work and traditional family roles.

Individual/Cultural Responsibility

Of course, shaming the homeless into making better decisions might be possible if homelessness and poverty were purely the result of individual choices. When people see homelessness as an individual choice, it is easy to situate homelessness and poverty as the end result of drugs, alcohol, mental illness, or unfortunate hardships. As noted by Smiley and West (2012), homelessness and poverty are socially positioned as a sign of personal failures and shortcomings and as a result "[t]he

54

poor have long been maligned, stereotyped, and disgraced as lazy, irresponsible leeches who are a detriment to society" (p. 72). Additionally, people who are homeless are often categorized as dirty, drunk, and depressed (Wasserman & Clair, 2010). By consistently analyzing personal addiction and illness as a cause for homelessness, people become blinded to several other macro-level contributing factors. As pointed out by Campbell and Reeves (1989), there are three main social factors that literally push people into homelessness: loss of jobs, absence of affordable housing, and gentrification of previously marginalized communities: i.e., pushing poor people out of their houses. Ultimately, a vast majority of U.S. Americans remain permanently disconnected from the poor and avoid discussions about how systems might be implicated in creating situations where poverty and homelessness are even a possibility. As a result, the housed and financially stable continue to position homelessness as a personal choice and are only concerned with how the poor are making efforts to help themselves get out of poverty (Wilson, 1996).

These ideas about the poor and homeless not only come from the housed and financially stable, but also from the poor and homeless populations. And some who are homeless or in poverty look beyond their own shortcomings to scapegoat other marginalized populations. For instance, when looking at poverty at the intersections of race, lower-class white Americans have pointed to illegal Mexican workers and overseas factory outsourcing to explain their own dire financial situations (Moss, 2003). In these examples, it is not the national or global marketplace systems that become the subjects of critique, but rather other lower-working-class people.

This is not to say that individual choices do not have a role in creating homelessness. However, individual choices are not solely responsible. Instead, it may be more appropriate to conceptualize homelessness as a vicious institution that is created and perpetuated through cultural interactions that are both individual and collective (Evans, 1988). These two positions feed off of one another and this dynamic interaction helps to demonstrate how we are all implicated in the existence of homelessness. In order to overcome the oppressive reality of homelessness, we need to formulate strong bonds across unyielding socio-economic class structures and work interdependently in an effort to hold both individual people and collective institutions accountable.

Arguably, it is difficult for many U.S. Americans to even comprehend the perennial state of homelessness because many people genuinely believe that people can make it out of poverty if they just try hard enough (Scott & Leonhardt, 2005). This notion of class mobility creates a deafening void where no one wants to talk about social class because no one wants to confront the notion that permanent inequities are still operating in twenty-first century U.S. America. Humorously noted, Fussell (1992) mentions that "actually, you reveal a great deal about your social class by the amount of annoyance or fury you feel when the subject is brought up" (p. 16). To his list of feelings, I would add the word "discomfort." Today, many people believe in class mobility, but as we begin to look at the issue of homelessness from a more collective vantage point, we can better understand how multiple factors contribute to a person ending up on the streets.

To begin, several factors including education, healthcare, housing, and public policy lead to the growing gap between the wealthy and those in poverty or on the brink of poverty (Noah, 2012). It is not one issue that drives poverty and homelessness, but a collection of issues unequally weighted in a complex matrix that is forever shifting the rules of the game. For example, cities are constantly looking for new ways to relocate homeless populations through ever-changing regulations. In these "clean-up" acts, cities have criminalized vagrancy by issuing citations and arresting homeless people for such minor offenses as panhandling, jaywalking, littering, smoking, sleeping in public, open alcohol containers, and abandoning debris (e.g. boxes, clothing) (Feldman, 2004; Flaccus, 2012). Markedly, the term "vagrancy" has certain negative connotations. I am not condoning or condemning its use, but simply using it to parallel the language that is used in crafting public policy and public discussions.

In Newport Beach, California, the public library "recently updated a policy that says staff can evict someone for having poor hygiene or a strong aroma" (Flaccus, 2012, para. 10). While these types of policies cannot explicitly target the homeless in the ordinances' language, and public officials continually insist that targeting the homeless is not their intention, many homeless people and advocates view various "clean-up" acts as directly targeting and disproportionately affecting the homeless populations (Flaccus, 2012; "Homeless Camping," 2012; Pearce, 2012; Stier, 2012).

In all of the efforts made to police certain types of public activities, perhaps none are as contentious as those policies that stipulate rules for public feeding. For example, the city of Philadelphia is currently fighting a civil rights lawsuit in an effort to prohibit people (volunteer groups, churches, etc.) from serving meals in city parks (Prois, 2012; Winkler & Gillespie, 2012) and Dallas already requires a person to obtain "official permission" before giving away food (Pearce, 2012, para. 2). In 2012, Mayor Michael Bloomberg pushed legislation that banned all food donations to New York City homeless shelters citing health concerns and nutrition guidelines ("Bloomberg Bans," 2012; Stier, 2012). In all, there are some cases where citations and regulations seem reasonable: for instance, city ordinances that issue fines in an effort to curb public urination or public intoxication. However, by and large, many ordinances seem to deliberately target non-threatening activities of the homeless who have nowhere else to sleep, eat, obtain finances, or store their belongings.

In comparison to such overt forms of public policy aimed at disciplining the behaviors of the homeless, there are also more covert forms of management when various political groups seek to purge the unsightly homeless from public spaces. For instance, during the 2008 Democratic National Convention (DNC) in Denver, Colorado, the planning committee moved to "secure 500 free movie tickets to provide temporary refuge for homeless people who might be uprooted by convention activities" (Katz, 2008, para. 3). Notably, the movie tickets were purchased by the DNC after their original plan—a plan that provided the homeless with day-passes to the Denver Zoo—fell through. While the DNC denied that these actions were taken in an effort to clear the homeless out of large parks for which the DNC had secured permits, it remains troubling that a political convention scheduled at the brink of an economic recession would encourage the homeless to leave convention activities through pacifying incentives as opposed to encouraging the homeless to take part in convention activities: specifically, those activities that deal with economic, poverty, and housing policies.

While instances of displacing the homeless are not always the direct result of political planning committees, homeless people can still be displaced when powerful political groups come to town. Unlike 2008, the 2012 DNC did not encourage the homeless to leave Charlotte, North Carolina with movie tickets and zoo passes. Instead, the economic boom caused by the onslaught of the 2012 DNC being held in Charlotte indirectly resulted in homeless people being removed or financially forced out of their temporary motel rooms to make room for delegates (Jamieson, 2012). As one homeless person reported, "Daily rates shot up from $30 a night to $300 a night" (Jamieson, 2012, para. 7). With such a drastic increase in rates, many homeless people and families were forced into shelters or onto the streets because they simply could not afford to absorb the higher costs that were being driven by temporary gentrification.

This is not to say that all political action is apathetic to the plight of the homeless or to suggest that politicians always turn a blind eye. In fact, there are those instances when political policy is intentionally designed to deal precisely with the issue of homelessness in a meaningful, compassionate way. However, as we will see, many of these programs fall flat and result in little change because the policies are misguided and crafted by public officials who have little understanding about the culture of homelessness. Illustrating this point is a case that centers on the Times Square Business Improvement District. In short, the Business Improvement District invested $2.5 million to create a one-year program intended to move hundreds of homeless people out of Times Square and into independent housing (MacDonald, 2000). This multi-layered program hired caseworkers to make contact with the homeless, develop relationships, and set up facilities for healthcare and shelter. On the surface it seemed like a winning solution for everyone: Times Square businesses no longer had to worry about loitering or vagrancy and people who were homeless would get the resources they needed to transition into a home. Yet, after a year of work, only *two* people had successfully transitioned from being homeless to having permanent shelter (MacDonald, 2000). Like many programs, the Times Square Business Improvement District invested lots of money, time, and effort into housing the homeless and experienced negligible outcomes.

As frustrating as these outcomes are, there are actually a few reasonable explanations that justify these results. First, there are no universal standards that translate between government and charitable agencies. Therefore, people who are homeless can simply leave one program for another if they do not like the varying requirements of work, addiction counseling, mental health counseling, or health screenings that one agency might demand (Olasky, 1992). In framing the fruitlessness of the Times Square Business Improvement District, it can be theorized that the homeless population around Times Square did not take full advantage of this specific program because they could receive similar services from other agencies that did not require them to look for a job, get health screenings, or maintain a drug-free lifestyle. Like many people, the homeless often take the path of least resistance when it comes to obtaining the services they need in order to maintain their current lifestyle. Forcing work and counseling requirements onto people who have no current interest in work or counseling simply drives those individuals to other agencies that provide them with shelter and food with no additional requirements. Therefore, without universal criteria for receiving services, many homeless people will continue to strategically navigate their way from agency to agency in a way that may not help them get into permanent housing, but does allow them to avoid work and counseling services for the time being (Olasky, 1992).

Second, some housing programs fail to produce tangible results because the homeless are sometimes "subsidized to not obtain the skills and make the sacrifices necessary to obtain such housing, when substandard accommodation is available free" (Schiff, 1990, p. 35). When looking at those homeless individuals who suffer from addiction disorders, the shelter system in its current form can actually hurt addicts' chances of getting help. This claim is based on research that illustrates how some homeless addicts choose to use their government subsidies for drugs and alcohol instead of using the monies for their intended purpose (food and shelter) because food and shelter are provided for free through other government and charitable organizations (Olasky, 1992). Notably, the government does not give out undirected cash to any person—homeless or non-homeless—receiving government welfare, and most people receive their food stamp benefits on an Electronic Benefit Transfers (EBT) card. However, a current report from the Government Accountability Institute does outline how EBT cards and housing vouchers are easily sold and traded online for cash through websites like Craigslist and Backpage (Hall, 2012; "Profits from Poverty," 2012). Additionally, while EBT cards cannot be used to purchase non-food items directly, "a database of 200 million Electronic Benefit Transfers records from January 2011 to July 2012" highlighted that EBT cards were being used to withdraw cash from ATMs inside bars, liquor stores, tobacco shops, porn shops, strip clubs, and casinos (Briquelet, 2013, para. 3).

On the surface, this analysis may sound accusatory and judgmental; however, when offering monetary benefits to populations that have disproportionately high numbers of people with mental health and addiction disorders, as well as disproportionately low numbers of educational achievement and marketable skills, it becomes increasingly valuable to look critically and honestly at habits and incentives. Additionally, these observations are not highlighted in this research to place blame on those who find themselves in poverty and/or homeless, but instead to highlight the failed structural relationship between those who need benefits and the agencies that wish to help them. In the end, programs that work do not "accept excuses, and [have] an emphasis on work and responsibility" (Olasky, 1992, pp. 214–215). People need to be given the opportunity to earn self-respect (Murray, 2012) and it would be advantageous to continue analyzing the types of organizational models that foster a successful transition from homelessness to housing.

Survival

While these "tough love" stances represent one end of the spectrum in addressing homelessness, the other end of the spectrum includes those who take a "hands off" approach and romanticize the homeless as free spirits (Feldman, 2004). In discussing homelessness, these free spirit accounts idealize the homeless for their resistance to dominant discourses about housing and living arrangements. For example, before the 1980s there was little media coverage given to homelessness, and the few articles that did appear in print categorized homelessness as "vagrancy" (Campbell & Reeves, 1989). Connotatively, the term "vagrancy" implies a choice to live life as a wandering hobo who loves a carefree lifestyle, or perhaps disrespect for the "need" for work. This mythical Americana character reemerged in popular culture throughout the 1990s as a kind of throwback to Kerouac's *On the Road* and the Beat generation. In short, "no home" translated into "living outside the system" during the hobo punk movement of the 1990s (DePastino, 2003, p. 265). This movement revered homelessness and thought it cool to hop trains and live as a nonconformist on the margins of society. Yet, like most movements that rely on the appropriation of marginalized others, this movement was co-opted by popular culture: publications such as *GQ, Maxim*, and *New York Times Magazine* eventually produced articles that celebrated the exhilarating homeless lifestyle and even commercialized the clothing fashion of train-hopping hoboes (DePasinto, 2003).

The obvious problem with idealizing homelessness in popular culture is that these types of representations fail to contextualize the notion of choice. In no uncertain terms, for those who find themselves homeless against their will, homelessness is a brutal struggle for everyday survival, not an exciting adventure for nonconforming teenagers and college students who always have the choice to go back home. This notion of survival is not simply limited to food, water, and shelter, but also surviving the violent culture that can arise within homeless spaces (Ravenhill, 2008). Within the context of homelessness, violence can manifest in a multitude of different ways. The most obvious manifestation is physical violence. For example, sleeping on the streets or at a shelter among large groups of other surviving people can leave a person vulnerable to violence as an attacker attempts to acquire what little property a person may have. While these acts do not always result in physical harm, the mental anguish of having to constantly guard or replace one's personal property can create massive amounts of daily stress, which may exacerbate physical health problems. Other forms of violence can include harm to self through destructive coping strategies, such as substance abuse or cutting (Walsh, 1992).

To survive this violence, small groups or partnerships may form alliances. In their article "'You've gotta learn how to play the game,'" Huey and Berndt (2008) draw attention to the gendered and sexualized roles women perform in homeless spaces as a means of acquiring male protection. Positioning homeless spaces as masculine spaces, women reported that they often use sex or sexual favors as a means of survival. Essentially, women find it more desirable to sexually attach themselves to one man (with whom they may or may not want to be sexually active) instead of being abused or raped by multiple men. Conversely, sometimes sexual abuse is what drives women to become homeless in the first place. For example, Peaches was a woman who became homeless in her attempt to escape an abusive relationship. She eventually made her way into a shelter where "the sheets that I got to put on the little wafer-thin mattress was bloody. When you shook out the sheets there was mice turds in it.... When they served food, you had a plate, you didn't have utensils" (Shipler, 2005, p. 153). In the end, Peaches left the shelter and returned to the man who abused her. Thus, even in those instances where a woman can navigate through the homeless system without feeling the pressures of sex for protection, the sometimes-abhorrent conditions of shelter life may make it more desirable to return to an abusive relationship.

For those men, women, and children who choose to stay at shelters, another hurdle to overcome is figuring out how to cope with the loss of privacy. In her book *21st Century Essays on Homelessness*, Anderberg (2011) situates the lack of privacy as so important that it is discussed in chapter one, "The Privilege of Privacy." Recalling her own experiences as a homeless person, Anderberg (2011) exposes the reader to a world where her homeless body was always on public display. To this end, she never felt as if she could relax or let her guard down. The desire for privacy also creates a grand contradiction for receiving help. On one hand, people who are homeless need to be publically outed as homeless in order to receive public assistance. On the other hand, people who are homeless value their privacy and wish to keep their homeless status confidential for many reasons, including guilt and shame.

Illustrating the particular theme of privacy, one can discover a vast amount of well-intentioned books, articles, and internet images that are extremely personal and arguably problematic. For instance, the book *Homeless in America* showcases several images of families in their most intimate moments in dire situations (Evans, 1998). One image in particular captures a mother and a father laying their infant child in a crib in the middle of a gymnasium overtaken with families and cots. Even more intimate is a picture of an older man's fully nude backside as he stands under a communal shower surrounded by wheelchairs and bed-frames that are pushed into the corner (Evans, 1998). While these pictures may have been intended to shock the reader into a deeper and more compassionate understanding of the harsh realities of homelessness, they not only depict, but geometrically exacerbate, the complete lack of privacy people have when engaging with family or using the bathroom. In the end, foregoing modesty and relinquishing privacy can sometimes be the heavy price that is paid in order to use public spaces for sleeping, eating, defecating, and showering—as well as the price of having one's image used for activism.

This lack of privacy may be why some people who find themselves impoverished resist the shelter systems and therefore, circumvent additional public aid that may otherwise enable them and their children to break the cycle of poverty. Avoiding public assistance not only hurts those who need assistance, but also provides governmental and charitable agencies with inaccurate statistics, hindering public efforts to provide adequate assistance. In her book *A Roof Over My Head*, Williams (2003) writes about women with children who avoid the shelter system as a means of resistance. In short, this resistance can be a stubborn claim of independence from negligent fathers, dismissive family members, or patronizing agencies.

There is also the issue of safety. This idea is further elaborated in Walsh's (1992) *Moving to Nowhere*, as she recalls the stories of families (both one-parent and two-parent) who avoid the shelter system as a way to protect their children from the stress and abuse that can happen within communal settings. Unfortunately, this continual avoidance of public services such as shelters, job placement agencies, and food pantries can perpetuate the cycle of poverty as families attempt to survive solely within the monetary welfare system (Williams, 2003). Breaking the cycle of poverty is difficult and requires both personal and financial assistance. Regrettably, some people are not receiving the full benefits of the system.

In the event that single mothers do seek help, their stories are often invisible in the public discourse against the strong stereotyped images of homeless people as older, single men. As DePastino (2003) writes, "Homeless women remain comparatively 'hidden' precisely because they have more available housing options, especially if they have children in tow" (p. 261). Essentially, people see more single men who are homeless because single men are more likely to live on the streets. Therefore, people disregard the possibility that single mothers with children could also be homeless because mothers with children are more likely to be hidden away in temporary housing. While these family images of homelessness may remain hidden from public view, Edin estimates that "more children are poor today than at any time since before Lyndon Johnson's War on Poverty began three decades ago" (cited in Wilson, 1996, p. 91). Regarding families, more recent research indicates that "homeless families increased 28 percent, from 131,000 in 2007 to 168,000 in 2010" (Smiley & West, 2012, p. 47).

Volunteerism

Up until this point, most of the discussion throughout this section has been focused on the cultural complexities that contextualize the homeless population. Yet, in discussing the homeless, it is also important to include a brief conversation about the volunteers who aspire to help those in need. As described by Cloke, Johnsen, and May (2007), the volunteers who intentionally place their bodies into this system do so with noble motivations and oftentimes are doing so from a place of care. As social workers, volunteers, and agencies look for ways to best help those who are homeless, they genuinely strive for creating caring environments where people can obtain help, feel safe, and feel humanized. Moreover, the need for these volunteers will continue to increase if the "current political and economic trends continue" (Lundahl & Wicks, 2010, p. 284).

Nevertheless, there are barriers within the current volunteer model that come from a lack of resources, the mismanagement of resources, or lack of knowledge about sufficient resources. Overall, homeless people disproportionately lack basic access to medical treatment, education, and job skills (Miller, Donahue, Este, & Hofer, 2004). As agencies and shelters are overrun with people needing assistance and understaffed by those who can provide assistance, homelessness soon becomes an issue of "crisis management" and the "containment of roofless people" (Ravenhill, 2008, p. 71). In this regard, volunteers and homeless shelters do a fairly adequate job in meeting clothing and food needs. However, volunteers and homeless shelters do a poor job in addressing deeper needs that could lead to independence through job training and education (Lundahl & Wicks, 2010). If there is any hope of homeless people escaping the system, then they need education and job skills that will allow them to perform in the mainstream workforce (Shipler, 2005).

Finally, it is important to continue analyzing how the current volunteer model works in an effort to be sure that the homeless population is being treated with dignity and respect. This is not to say that volunteers intentionally disrespect homeless people; however, it should be noted that some gestures of charity can sometimes be interpreted as condescending and infantilizing. For example, in describing the distribution of food to those who are hungry, Wasserman and Clair (2010) use the term "drive-by feeding" (p. 191). Implicit in this term are three key factors. First, there are many people who need food quickly. Second, the people who distribute food must do so quickly in order to feed as many hungry people as possible. Third, while this quick-feeding system may cure temporary hunger, it does not provide a model where the distributors can engage with the hungry on an intimate level and form deep interpersonal relationships. Essentially, this model neglects the aspect of human interaction and avoids any consideration for reciprocation. Consequentially, people receiving services are always positioned as "those in need" while volunteers are always positioned as "those with services."

Instead, volunteers and the homeless should work in a mutually beneficial manner where homeless people are equally treated as having services of value. In the end, homeless people should be provided services from volunteers in exchange for partaking in varying responsibilities around the shelter or the community (MacDonald, 2000). Without such conditions, homeless people become forever dependent on the goodwill of volunteers and are never placed in a position where they are expected to harness their abilities and gain independence. Until social services, agencies, and institutions insist on homeless people participating in their own uplift, personal empowerment remains impossible and job skills are prone to atrophy.

As a complex issue, confronting homelessness will require a complex solution. In recognizing the complexity of homelessness, politicians and scholars cannot succumb to the notion that confronting homelessness is as simple as budgeting additional money for food, shelter, healthcare, and counseling services. As discussed earlier, extraordinary amounts of money have been appropriated for programs and services over the past five decades in an effort to end poverty and homelessness with effectively zero change in the proportional number of people who remain in poverty and/or homeless. Obviously, "a civilized society does not let its people starve in the streets" (Murray, 1984, p. 16) and I am not advocating draconian budget cuts to services and programs for the poor. However, there are growing cases of ineptitude, incompetence, and ineffectiveness in the system that make it increasingly difficult for the poor and/or homeless to receive services that are adequate in addressing the source of the problem. Returning to Black-well (2012), "Yes, there can be a downside to ever greater government provision. Many things done in the name of compassion—even compassionate conservatism—can have undesirable side effects" (para. 2). In this vein, homelessness and poverty are systemic issues that go far deeper than an individual lack of funds.

While I have great respect for those who have devoted countless hours to creating the current wealth of scholarship, the one glaring gap I have found within the discipline is the lack of in-depth research where the multiple voices of those who are homeless are highlighted and positioned at the center of cultural, social, economic, and housing conversations. Instead of listening to the insights of homeless people, we more often hear from experts arguing about how to deal with the homeless as third-party subjects. Notably, homelessness is an issue that has little direct impact on the daily realities of these experts, whereas *expert analysis does have major consequences for the daily realities of those who are homeless.* Therefore, scholarship should address homelessness in a manner that will create larger academic platforms where those individuals who face the vicious cycle of homelessness have the opportunity to share their experiences in their own voices. Ultimately, scholars must be willing to embrace the narratives of the homeless as sources of valuable knowledge that can help create better-informed public policy in an effort to develop more effective solutions.

4. The Case for Narratives

While living in Camden, I got to know many people who were homeless. One of those people was Bobby. I first met Bobby at a Dunkin' Donuts where he insistently asked for $7 so that he could buy a bus ticket to Trenton—about a 45-minute drive north. The story was that he had recently been accepted to a drug-treatment center and needed to get out of Camden before he started using again. I reluctantly gave Bobby the money (fearing that he would not spend it on his stated purpose), but held some hope that he would get the help he needed. Within a week, I saw Bobby back at the shelter in Camden. He was strung-out with no place to go. I was disappointed, but not overly surprised. My personal rule is that I will help any homeless person who needs help with no questions asked as long as we maintain an open and honest relationship. However, once a person burns me, the trust is lost and I move on. It may seem coldhearted, but I cannot in good conscience enable a person's abusive drug habit by blindly giving him money based on sad, yet untrue, stories.

Bobby ignored me for a few months, knowing that I was no longer any good for scrap cash. When he finally did approach, he wasn't looking for a handout, but wanted to make an honest trade. In short, he was offering to sell his $300 food stamp card for $150 cash. He didn't try to hide the fact that he would to use the $150 for crack cocaine and I wasn't overly concerned about the moral implications of a middle-aged crack addict trying to sell his government benefits. What struck me was the apparent ease with which the welfare system could be manipulated. To be sure this wasn't an anomaly, I checked with several other homeless people in the neighborhood. Sure enough, the practice of selling, trading, and pawning food stamps, welfare checks, and housing vouchers was a common practice in the streets.

As a scholar, volunteer, and taxpayer, I am annoyed at how effortlessly government benefit systems can be manipulated. However, I am not morally aghast with poor people who "inappropriately" use government assistance to survive the harsh realities of poverty. If anything, Bobby's story is useful in illustrating how many people—whether homeless or housed—use broken systems to their advantage. In looking at the homeless community, these broken systems may be used to obtain drugs or increased benefits, just as the housed community may use these broken systems to evade taxes or avoid high-interest loan rates.

In researching the culture of homelessness, a major concern is that government programs are unknowingly supporting addiction and dependency by supplying useless benefits, such as food stamps, to people *who have no kitchens*. Therefore, a person's ability to mobilize himself out of homelessness may become inhibited by lax government programs that unintentionally encourage people to misappropriate benefits on unhealthy lifestyle choices. In all the places I have worked and traveled, the vast majority of homeless people know where to find free food through soup kitchens and food pantries. With their food needs met, some, like Bobby, choose to use their food stamp cards to barter for other services. Confronting this reality is important in order to reshape policies to more accurately address the experiences of homeless people. Only then can we create systems that will actually help people get off the streets. One way of achieving this is by listening to the narratives of homeless people.

Within the study of rhetoric, various scholars have made the claim that human beings construct their lives through narrative (Williams, 2007). In doing so, these scholars have helped construct what is known as the narrative paradigm. In all, the narrative paradigm prioritizes narratives as a way to gather knowledge. In this research, the personal stories of homeless individuals are validated and affirmed as well as compassionately considered when crafting public policy. In telling Bobby's story, it is not the objective to judge desperate actions or make arguments for cutting services for the poor and the homeless. Instead, the objective is to illustrate the considerable disconnect between the intentions of those who provide assistance and the actual effects on those who receive assistance. While those who provide assistance are doing so in an effort to help the homeless find housing and sustain independent living, these provisions have thus far been ineffective and homeless rates have remained unchanged over the past 50 years (see

Murray, 1984; Olasky, 1992; Smiley & West, 2012). Perhaps the unspoken reason for this stagnation is that, by and large, people who are homeless remain unheard in a society that tries to collectively diagnose the problem, craft the solution, and study the outcome.

By recounting Bobby's story, his narrative is positioned as an important voice to be heard in the fight to end homelessness. As a group, the narratives of homeless people are effectively ignored in public conversations about government benefits. Instead, the vociferous voices of politicians and scholars who are not homeless direct the conversation. Yet, listening to stories from the homeless is crucial because homeless people receive government assistance and their voices can tell non-homeless people whether or not the assistance is helpful. In this vein, the narrative paradigm provides a framework where firsthand knowledge about homelessness is equally valued to the knowledge of individuals who write benefit policy. If scholars are willing to accept the stories of the homeless as a site of knowledge production, then perhaps those who are concerned about helping the homeless can help create workable solutions that actually address the needs of the homeless, rather than financially supporting broken systems that unintentionally subsidize harmful behaviors and perpetuate homelessness.

Narrative Paradigm

The narrative paradigm was most completely articulated in Walter Fisher's 1984 article "Narration as a Human Communication Paradigm: The Case of Public Moral Argument." The purpose of Fisher's article was to create an academic paradigmatic shift that understood human communication through the process of making narratives. In doing so, the narrative paradigm combines traditional forms of argumentation and persuasion with literary and artistic elements of style (Fisher, 1984). Before rhetorical scholars fully articulated the narrative paradigm, they understood argumentation and persuasion by leaning heavily on the more traditional methods of what Fisher referred to as "the rational world paradigm." While Fisher continuously makes it clear that the rational world paradigm should not be entirely abandoned, he does indicate that it contains two glaring concerns.

First, traditional argumentation and persuasion skills must be taught. Second, varying degrees of argumentative skill can create a hierarchy among people. These concerns become problematic when people who lack these skills are dismissed during civic engagement (Hollis, 1977; Toulmin, 1970) because the rational world paradigm creates a system where those who have greater access to education and social status have pronounced civic advantages over those who do not. Without these educational or professional qualifications, the homeless (and other marginalized groups) have a hard time creating substantive arguments and are ignored in the public arena when their conclusions contradict the advice of so-called "experts." On the other hand, the narrative paradigm celebrates storytelling as a universal mode of communication that can create shared meaning and unity across cultures.

Additionally, the narrative paradigm presupposes that all people's experiences and stories should be given equal consideration based on the assumption that the act of narration has no rules that people must learn, but instead happens as a part of the human condition (Fisher, 1984). Essentially, the capacity for narration is something all people are born with and not a condition of educational and/or socio-economic status. By rejecting the dualism of modernity, the narrative paradigm welcomes multiple ways of knowing as well as multiple ways of moving through the world. Creating a space for the narrative paradigm also means that scholars are embracing new ways to cultivate knowledge and validate knowledge production. In moving toward the narrative paradigm, scholars are providing access for more people to share stories across boundaries in more meaningful and democratic ways.

On a personal level, communicating stories provides individuals the ability to give meaning to their lived experiences and pass these stories on to others. This process is described as "narrative-sensemaking," which "refers to the narrator's attempt to understand his or her experience more fully by engaging in the act of telling" (Montalbano-Phelps, 2004, p. 61; Bute & Jensen, 2011). While some people may use more technical or scientific jargon based on their field of study or career choice, the foundation for human communication is still rooted in a person's ability to narrate those experiences in such a manner as to have those experiences acknowledged and accepted by others. Ultimately, communication is rooted in historical and situational contexts where multiple narratives strive for validation and affirmation (Fisher, 1987).

Notably, there are concerns regarding the extent to which a narrative approach will bolster democracy, specifically for those with limited social and financial capital (Rowland, 1987). However, even under heavy skepticism, a narrative approach to debating public policy should be defended as one of the only ways where the homeless are at least given the opportunity to defend their experiences against the opinions of the elites. In contrast, the rational world paradigm requires a plethora of credentials before a person is even allowed into the conversation. For instance, try to think about the last time a homeless person was invited to speak in front of Congress, write an academic article, publish a memoir, or even contribute to the board meeting of his local homeless shelter. Now think about how often non-homeless experts are invited into these spaces.

In the end, the rational world paradigm celebrates experts who are nearly infallible, compared to those who are not learned in the skills of argumentation. Yet, knowledge is also found in the personal narratives of the homeless. Certainly, this does not presuppose that the opinions of the homeless are always correct. A narrative approach simply asks that all perspectives are considered before a solution is agreed to—and if a person cannot articulate his perspective via traditional argumentation, he should be allowed to offer arguments through personal narrative. Whereas, the rational world paradigm oftentimes creates winners and losers solely based on one's ability to argue *according to its rules*, the narrative paradigm recognizes that knowledge production is not necessarily linear and a person's ability to argue does not automatically mean that he is correct.

Narratives and Homelessness

As will be illustrated in the following examples, by embracing narrative, researchers are placed in a position that allows them to more fully understand the social problems and personal obstacles that plague underrepresented groups. Perhaps the most prominent theme is that behind the population statistics and financial numbers are people wrestling with emotional turmoil. As Montalbano-Phelps (2004) comments on narratives, "people tell stories to survive" (p. 1). As a model for survival, narratives help people negotiate a variety of difficult situations.

For example, in looking at the narratives of former middle-class individuals who were hit especially hard by the 2008 recession, Van De Mieroop (2011) describes the process by which these former middle-class individuals shifted and evolved their personal stories to reflect the reality that they were now a part of the lower class. This transition into a new economic identity can be both painful and revealing and cannot necessarily be captured through statistics that quantify median incomes and national foreclosures. However, documenting these transitions through narrative does allow others to empathize and more closely consider the immediate implications of public policy.

Regarding homelessness, narration allows people to speak through their experiences in a way that can uncover hidden beliefs, meanings, and sense of self. While even the homeless may not understand the policy significance of capturing their narratives, over time people begin to more deeply understand their identities, their wants, and their goals. In turn, this leaves open the possibility of narrating oneself out of seemingly hopeless situations. Without narrating these experiences, people can remain stuck in undesirable situations because of ignorance. It is only when narration takes place that a person can move from a pattern of disempowered helplessness to active empowerment (Montalbano-Phelps, 2004).

Reflecting on the role of scholars who collect narratives from underrepresented groups, Duneier (2001) cautions that the gathering can be both emotionally uplifting and emotionally draining since such intimate contact can cause a scholar to become emotionally attached to the participants. In discussing his life's work as a professional listener, Studs Terkel (1993) was fully aware that his approach in collecting narratives was voyeuristic in nature; however, many people he interviewed freely talked about their hardships and triumphs without apparent filters because Terkel's motives remained open and transparent. Furthermore, Terkel (1993) was direct in displaying passion for his work. In his book *Division Street America*, Terkel's (1993) goal was to show the reader that the lives of everyday Chicagoans were not dull and boring but full of vibrant and colorful wisdom that produced valuable knowledge. Terkel was positioned not as an author, but as a good listener with a gift for asking the right questions.

Before *Division Street America*, Terkel (1970) collected narratives of poverty in *Hard Times: An Oral History of the Great Depression*. In his opening statements, Terkel (1970) writes, "This is not a lawyer's brief nor an annotated sociological treatise. It is simply an attempt to get the story of the holocaust known as The Great Depression from an impoverished battalion of survivors" (p. 3). Wrapped within these thoughts is the notion that poor people have stories and that their stories play a vital role in helping to shape a more complete historical account of the Great Depression. Extending poor people's narratives beyond the historical significance of the Great Depression, it ought to be added that such story telling can help poor people make sense of difficult situations, as well as provide financially-stable people with a more complete view of the emotional and cultural differences that exist within stratified economies.

Two other scholars who took it upon themselves to document firsthand accounts of the poor are Conover and Kozol. Conover's (1984) unique look at poverty occurred through his ethnographic approach to train-hopping (an attempt to experience the life of hoboes and "leather-tramps," in reference to worn shoe leather from walking). While this lifestyle may appear romantic at first, Conover (1984) is relentless in describing this transient existence as harsh with "no social mobility, no safety, nobody to count on, [and] nobody to love. Tramps were strangers wherever they went. Living with them had made me homesick, period" (p. 280). Through this widely-published book, the experiences of hoboes were given public attention and the narratives of hoboes were provided the opportunity to be heard and considered in public spaces.

As for Kozol (2006), his appropriately titled book *Rachel and Her Children* vividly records the narratives of homeless families as they attempt to negotiate an uncompromising maze of social services and government assistance. In documenting these narratives, Kozol illustrates the tremendous cultural disconnect between those who are homeless and those who are housed. For example, Kozol (2006) interviews mothers who claim additional children or children with disabilities (sometimes fictional disabilities) in order to receive different benefits; corner store owners who allow patrons to buy diapers with food stamps for an extra surcharge even though non-food items are not supposed to be purchased with food stamps; and people who use the library for shelter when no other options are available. These library dwellers get unsympathetically thrown out when they are caught sleeping.

The value of these narratives is not found in the ethical imperative as to whether or not homeless people are using the system "correctly." Instead, the value of these narratives is that they help readers gain a more accurate understanding of the dysfunctional relationship between the homeless and those who offer assistance. These stories are compelling precisely because they allow homeless people to articulate their positionality within the welfare system. Thus, drawing attention to a broken, wasteful, and sometimes useless welfare system. Documenting these stories gives homeless people the opportunity to have a dyadic conversation with the politicians and volunteers who are in charge of divvying up assistance. If politicians and volunteers listen to these stories, then perhaps they will be in a better position to help homeless people achieve the shared objectives of increased permanent housing and increased independent living. Ignoring these stories will only perpetuate welfare systems that are not working very effectively.

In addition to scholars' accounts, there are also some instances where the homeless are speaking on their own behalf. For example, homeless people have written books (Anderberg, 2011), poetry (Finley, 2010), and edited newspapers (Lindemann, 2007). Although their circulation is limited, these texts work together to provide an opportunity for homeless people to speak directly to the general public, including scholars, journalists, advocates, and politicians, in a way that validates their experiences and lends credibility to their embodied knowledge. Additionally, these stories can help challenge dominant discourses about homelessness and work to create alliances across socio-economic and educational barriers. Homeless people matter and their stories should be heard. In an effort to create more opportunities for the homeless to share their stories, those with access to voice need to continually highlight the stories of homeless people and demonstrate how these stories are essential components in shaping public policy.

Collecting Narratives

I left Camden in 2007 to pursue graduate degrees at Central Michigan University and then Southern Illinois University. During the next six years of school, I remained active as a volunteer among the homeless populations in my respective communities. I volunteered at soup kitchens and shelters and even spent time driving people to court dates and social services appointments. Near the end of graduate school, I began reaching out to faculty members about a direction for my dissertation. I was already engaged in the issue of homelessness as a volunteer and avid student, but I wasn't sure how to make the transition into formal researcher. I had read copious amounts of other scholars' research as well as plenty of political policy papers from conservatives, liberals, and everyone in between. Yet, even after all this reading, I didn't know how I might contribute to the ongoing academic discussions aimed at solving this complex social problem. In fact, it seemed as if everything important had already been said and every solution had already been proposed. What was the new research angle? However, by emphasizing the need for first-person narratives and experiences, this research was able to focus in on three primary questions that were oftentimes overlooked:

R1: How do homeless people narrate their experiences?

R2: What types of experiences and relationships do homeless people have with government benefits and charitable organizations?

R3: How would homeless people craft economic and social policy if given the opportunity to do so?

To help answer these questions, three basic methods were utilized: ethnography, observation, and interviewing. Ethnography originated in anthropology as a way to become more familiar with a culture's social practices. The objective of researchers who use ethnography is to "try to immerse themselves in a setting and become part of the group being investigated, in order to understand the meanings that actors put upon events or situations" (Iacono, Brown, & Holtham, 2009, p. 40). In an effort to better understand the culture of homelessness as well as gain trust within the community, make observations, and track down potential interviews, I continued working a 24-hour a week job at a local homeless shelter, Good Samaritan Ministries (also known as "Good Sam's") in Carbondale, Illinois. I also began spending time with the homeless in front of a popular bar hang-out, at a local park, and near popular intersections where several people panhandled. These situations created ideal conditions for detailing observations.

Good Sam's is a shelter that serves three meals a day and has room to accommodate 20–25 individuals in overnight, temporary housing. Temporary housing at Good Sam's means residents may stay up to 30 days at the shelter before they have to leave. Anyone is allowed to stay in temporary housing as long as he does not possess drugs or alcohol, fight, or have an arrest warrant issued against him. When people leave temporary housing, they cannot return for 30 days. Good Sam's also has transitional housing for 10–12 individuals. These residents may stay up to two years. Transitional housing has a tougher screening process and residents must apply to get into the program. In transitional housing, residents have their own rooms, are responsible for cooking and cleaning, enroll in educational courses, and receive help in locating and maintaining employment.

To better contextualize this specific shelter, it is important to understand the broader region's socio-economic situation. In January 2013, *The Southern Illinoisan* reported that Jackson County, which includes the city of Carbondale, had the highest poverty rate in Illinois at 33.7 percent (Norris, 2013). The increasing poverty level of Jackson County also meant that services would be in higher demand. For example, in 2012, Good Sam's estimated that a total of 28,000–29,000 meals would be served at its facility. These numbers indicated a 5,000–6,000 meal increase above what had been served in the previous year (Kulash, 2011). However, in September 2011, *The Southern Illinoisan* reported that while poverty in Illinois grew, the resources aimed at alleviating economic hardships had dwindled (Tareen, 2011). For example, from 2011 to 2012, the Illinois Department of Human Services (IDHS) cut $669.3 million from their budget (Tareen, 2011). Funding from IDHS subsidizes low-income housing, food assistance, and shelters. Good Sam's was affected by these budgetary shortfalls when they lost 52 percent of their government funding in one year (Mileur, 2011) and there was a 62 percent reduction in food bank assistance (Kulash, 2011). So far, these resources have not been replenished.

While Good Sam's was the primary location for data collection, the nature of this study did present situations where observations, interactions, and interviews took place in surrounding locations. For example, initial contact with two interviewees was made at Good Sam's, but by the time they were ready to be interviewed, they had passed their 30-day limit at the shelter. Therefore, it was arranged to interview these individuals in a public park about one mile from the shelter. Additionally, there were four participants who used Good Sam's for its food, restroom, and shower facilities, but these participants did not stay at Good Sam's overnight, either because they did not like to stay at the shelter or because they were banned. In these instances, plans were made to meet these participants at various locations around town.

Ultimately, data for this study was collected over a period of three months: May 15, 2013–August 15, 2013. Throughout the study, I worked at Good Sam's 24 hours per week and spent an additional five hours per week with homeless people at the park, in front of the bar, or at popular street intersections. Being in these spaces allowed me to "note the relationship between cultural reconstructions and the physical environments in which [participants] live" (Carspecken, 1996, p. 203). During this time, observations were noted, field notes were taken, and informal interactions were had that allowed for a better understanding of the environmental context, as well as foster good relationships.

The formal interviewing process did not begin until the second month. In total, it took two months (June 2013–August 2013) to recruit 10 participants and conduct 10 interviews (see Appendix A for a list of participants and demographic information). These 10 interviews lasted from 28 minutes and 56 seconds to 64 minutes and 11 seconds and were conducted at Good Sam's, the town square, a local recreation center, McDonald's, and two different parking lots. As Gubrium and Holstein (2012) write, "Narrative environments not only feed personal accounts but are also a source of socially relevant questions that interviewers pose to respondents" (p. 39). Therefore, during each interview the uniqueness of the surroundings prompted relevant questions about living at the shelter, living on the streets, and relationships with the community. Additionally, because many of these locations were where homeless people gathered, stayed, or panhandled, participants had the opportunity to point to and indicate the locations they were referencing: e.g., bedrooms, showers, park benches, restaurants where they used the restrooms, hotels they would stay at when they had the money, and awnings under which they slept. While there were guiding questions for the interviews (see Appendix B), the direction of the interviews were allowed to evolve naturally. In the end, interviews strove to proceed through all of the questions in a manner that encouraged the participants to set the tone as well as take ownership of their stories.

Narrative Analysis

In analyzing the data, it was important to remember that the conclusions would be imperfect and incomplete. Addressing this concern, Denzin (1997) writes:

> Ethnographies will not attempt to capture the totality of a group's way of life. The focus will be interpreted slices, glimpses, and specimens of interactions that display how cultural practices, connected to structural formations and narrative texts, are experienced at a particular time and place by interacting individuals [p. 247].

Because of the desire to capture *everything*, honing in on one mode of analysis was a difficult task. Did *I* want to focus on ideology and politics? Did *I* want to focus on gender and race? Did *I* want to focus on economics and poverty? After stepping back, I came across some notes from Becker's (1986) *Writing for Social Scientists*. In this book, Becker (1986) reminds scholars that *researchers are not the sole producers of their texts* and that writing up observations is a collective act. Therefore, it ought not to be the objective to artificially drive the analysis, but to record what is observed, type up notes, and allow the themes to emerge organically.

In the end, Pelias (2011) reminds us that scholarly "work is always partial and partisan" (p. 664). Narrative analysis is partial because interpretations are never final and research can always be reordered, rearranged, and restructured. Narrative analysis is partisan because researchers enter the field with ideological biases and lived histories that influence what they observe and how they observe. Therefore, the analysis that follows recognizes the limitations of this research's subjectivity in an effort to minimize faulty generalizations (Minnich, 1986) and to remain open to competing dialogue and different interpretations. In working toward more inclusive scholarship, this research attempts to allow the experiences of the participants to drive the emergent themes and continuously works at placing the voices of the participants at the center of the scholarship.

By the end of the analysis, the hope is to have created an academic account of homelessness that is critical, reflexive, and rooted in the narratives of those who live these vulnerable realities every day. Prior to this research, the most powerful narratives I had heard about homelessness commented on the generalities of how homelessness forces people into a day-to-day struggle to exist (Rossi, 1989). There is stress in losing privacy, stress in finding shelter, stress in navigating the system, and stress that comes with the overall uncertainty with the direction of life. By designing a study where homeless people can discuss these issues more in-depth, perhaps narrative ownership and personal empowerment become possible. To this end, constantly pursing this type of personal-narrative-driven research might encourage other scholars, politicians, and social workers to generate more opportunities where those who are most affected by public conversations concerning economics, housing, food assistance, and social services will finally have a voice in those conversations.

5. Losing Everything

The difficulties that would be faced throughout the data collection process were immediately apparent. When beginning work at Good Sam's in May 2013, I was forward with the patrons about my long-term academic goals and how the objective was to learn more about how homeless people narrated their lived experiences. These initial conversations were casual, and besides, nothing formal would take place for another four weeks. Overall, people seemed generally intrigued in the research and appeared happily surprised that someone was taking an academic interest in bringing attention to homelessness. However, while explaining that there was a need for collecting personal interviews, people would often respond with a sarcastic "good luck" and became visibly hesitant and distanced.

Ultimately, recruiting people into the project became a point of stress and caused me to second-guess the entire project. From a logistical standpoint, interviewing homeless people was agonizing. First, many of them lacked a personal phone and regular email access. So they were hard to get hold of or follow up with. Second, none of them had a consistent daily schedule and tracking down potential participants was challenging. Finally, because their lifestyles were so fluid, it was impossible to schedule interviewing appointments. Therefore, people had to be approached when I saw them and do interviews on-the-spot or the data collection process risked losing a potential participant. This also necessitated that all of the interviews take place in public spaces. While the participant and I would find a relatively private spot away from potential eavesdroppers, we could not control the noise and potential distractions caused by traffic, weather, and the occasional passersby.

These interviews also caused an ethical dilemma. Of course I had known several of my potential interviewees from working at Good

Sam's and hanging around the local areas where many of them congregated, but once the conversations turned personal, many people either passed or said, "I'll think about it." Once they said, "I'll think about it," it was realized that the person would never be interviewed. "I'll think about it" was simply the polite way of saying that the research dug too deeply into their personal business. In short, many people were reluctant to share their distressing stories and soon caused me to question the methodology and ethical responsibilities of collecting stories from such a vulnerable population. In quiet moments of humility it was realized that this research was essentially asking homeless people to talk to a stranger about what was, quite possibly, the most shame-filled aspect of their lives. They had already lost so much of their material lives, was it even ethical to ask them to also give up their private lives and thus, lose everything? In thinking about this book's earlier critiques of Evans' (1998) photography that exhibited homeless people during intensely personal moments, I began to question whether or not this research was prying too much.

In the end, this research continued to pry and I still remain conflicted about it. Yet, these ethical struggles over asking people to share their private stories did become a catalyst for better understanding the concept of "loss" within the homeless community. The remainder of this chapter attempts to capture these stories of loss in five areas. First, in addition to these prying questions regarding emotional openness, this chapter looks at other ways homeless people lose privacy. It also discusses the stories of loss surrounding jobs and finances. It examines the loss of physical health, safety, and material possessions. It summarizes how people who are homeless have lost their sense of family. And finally, it looks at how homeless people communicate a loss of self and self-worth.

Loss of Privacy

While collecting data, I was often reminded of Anderberg's (2011) personal narratives about being homeless and, in particular, her chapter "The Privilege of Privacy." This sentiment was never more tangible in the observation phase than during the intake process at Good Sam's. As a staff member, I was sometimes in charge of client intake and the intake process dictated that staff had to collect names, former addresses, social security numbers, physical and mental health histories, finances, and welfare benefit information. Additionally, staff had to administer drug tests through urine samples, alcohol tests through a breathalyzer, and contact the police department to inquire about any outstanding warrants. At this point in the process, Good Sam's now had information about personal histories as well as any current illicit behaviors. The final, and one of the more invasive acts of the intake process, was for staff members to collect and label medications. A locked cabinet that hung on the wall was filled with patrons' bags of medications and only the staff had access. Therefore, not only was the staff informed about what medications patrons took, but the staff also served as gatekeeper of those medications. Consequently, patrons could not access their private medications without permission. In all, a person's entire life was given to and catalogued by a stranger he or she had met within the first fifteen minutes of entering Good Sam's.

While the collection of personal information could be invasive, all patrons readily complied without ever raising a question about the validity of the process or whether the information would be kept private. However, interviewees did react to this process. As communicated by Tiffany:

> You go through a lot mentally getting shuffled all over the place. You lose your privacy and you start to realize what you've lost and it's hard. It's been really affecting me because I've lost my privacy for a while now. I have no privacy anymore. I mean, you've got your own room here, but they're not sound proof. The bathrooms, you've got to share with everybody and not everybody's clean. That's an issue. I mean, every staff member here knows everything about me and everybody else. It's hard when you lose your privacy.

Part of Tiffany's concern with privacy was the fact that she and her husband shared a room at Good Sam's. They were recently married and had been living at Good Sam's for 43 days at the time this interview took place. In the larger context of our discussion, it was evident that part of her frustration with the rooms not being "sound proof" had to do with her and her husband's desire for sexual intimacy.

The complexity of sexuality and privacy within the homeless community came up more than once during my time at Good Sam's. Twice a man complained to me that his roommate was up at night masturbating and once a resident complained about semen in the shower. Perhaps the most relevant incident of sexuality and privacy occurred when Jane was arrested and spent one week in jail for manually stimulating her boyfriend behind an outdoor shed. This incident is relevant because Jane's lack of privacy in expressing her sexuality created conditions where public resources (tax money to arrest and jail her) were used to stop her behavior. Whereas many housed people likely have similar sexual experiences in private, Jane's lack of privacy meant that her sexual experience was dealt with as a public problem and was eventually documented in the official public record.

While public displays of sexual intimacy are not a conundrum that every homeless person deals with, all homeless people do deal with the issue of having to use the restroom. When speaking with Kenneth, I learned that simply finding a restroom when homeless can be a site of public debate. As told by Kenneth, he was banned from using the McDonald's restroom because he smelled bad. He continued:

> Another guy came by and asked the McDonald's manager, "Hey, if I give him ten dollars, can he come in here and get something to eat?" And McDonald's said, "No, we don't want him in here." It was all because I used to go in there to use the bathroom and I smell bad. I know I smell bad. I'm out here in the sun all day and I can't take a shower and wash my clothes all the time. I try to when I can.... Well, I try to stay [at the hotel] as much as I can so I can take a shower every night. If I could do that, then I wouldn't have gotten banned from McDonald's.

While McDonald's is technically a privately-owned established and has no legal obligation to allow homeless people to use their restrooms, McDonald's (and other fast-food restaurants') restrooms are commonly the only spaces where homeless people can quickly and quietly use the restroom. Unfortunately, Kenneth now evacuates in public when he is not near Good Sam's or staying at a hotel. Hence, his private act became a public issue.

Ultimately, Kenneth's, Tiffany's, and Jane's stories are all reminders that even the most private moments for homeless people have public consequences and require public attention. For example, the police, sanitation department, or social services might be tasked with addressing any of the aforementioned situations. Of course, housed people are rarely subjected to public scrutiny regarding any of these activities because housed people are able to perform these activities in private. Furthermore, housed people are rarely asked to disclose personal information to strangers. Yet, because each of these homeless individuals must utilize public services, share public rooms, use public restrooms/bathrooms, and socialize in public parks, it becomes socially acceptable to ask for their private information and regulate their personal behaviors. *In short, homeless people have no privacy because they have no private property.* Instead, everything in their life is at risk of becoming public. In the end, homeless people's inability to experience or maintain guaranteed privacy creates a condition where their lives are always on public display and at the mercy of public critique.

Loss of Financial Stability

Sometimes, public critiques of the homeless transform into blaming homeless people for the situations in which they find themselves. Kenneth described some of the verbal abuse he received from people while he stood on the corner holding his cardboard sign:

> I'm always hollered at, "Get a job!" When they do it, they just drive by. I'd like to get one of them to stop and ask them, "How am I supposed to get a job when I keep putting in applications and no one wants to hire me and we got a high unemployment rate?" ... Like the people who yell, "Get a job!" I want to ask them, "Do you not watch the news? Do you not know that we have a high unemployment rate? You don't know me. You don't know that I put in my applications. You just know that I'm out here."

In writing about the homeless, Campbell and Reeves (1989) noted that the loss of jobs was one of the main reasons people found themselves homeless. In fact, six of the ten people interviewed said, losing a job (either theirs or a spouse's) was the reason they ended up homeless.

For example, before moving to Carbondale five years ago, Kenneth worked as a custodian at the Southern Illinois Miners' field, a local baseball team, where he "picked up trash and cleaned the bathrooms." He also worked part-time at a restaurant "for nine years delivering pizza." He lost both jobs around the time of the 2008 recession and he "lived off unemployment for the first couple of years; friends and family for a couple of years after that. And now [asking people for spare change] is finally a last resort." Unlike Kenneth, Ashley had not been working before she became homeless because of a back injury. However, her "husband had a job working with aluminum, but he got laid off" 18 months ago. Ashley and her husband, Philip, now spend their days standing at an intersection asking drivers for money.

Unfortunately, jobs were scarce in poverty-stricken Jackson County, Illinois, at the time this research was conducted. As Tiffany mentioned:

> Jackson County is so poor right now. I mean, if there's no one here anymore to help people with jobs, then there's going to be a lot more homeless people. Right now, no one has any work. People just need help or this world is going to be homeless.

However, according to Tiffany, there were some people who were getting jobs:

> I mean, this is a college town and it seems like [students are] first. College students get first everything.... I've got a bunch of friends who are college people and everybody just mingles, but college students always seem to get first dibs on jobs and housing. So if you don't have a job by now [August 1, 2013] or this weekend or next week, you might as well forget it.

For several interviewees and during observations, there seemed to be a quiet tension between the college students and the long-term Carbondale residents who struggled financially. Southern Illinois University sat in a privileged area of town where, according to Tiffany, "SIU students can just come and go and not worry about how much poverty is in other parts of Carbondale." The competition for low-wage jobs, such as servers and sales clerks, was not something Tiffany held against college students, but she did mention that "maybe holding open some of these jobs for homeless people is something that everyone [in Carbondale] should pay more attention to."

Certainly for many homeless people, struggles with employment are directly connected to struggles with housing. Before ending up on the street, married couple Philip and Ashley were making payments to a landlord in an effort to buy the trailer they were renting. As Philip told it:

> We used to live at [The Marshalls], but we got tricked out of [the trailer] because the manager at the time told us that he was trying to help us buy the trailer to own. The [Shepard] church even helped us get the down payment for it, but come to find out, [the landlord] was doing some shady stuff under the table. But we didn't know, so we kept making what we thought were payments, but then he kept coming up with another story about how we couldn't buy it that month or the next. Eventually our sewer backed up and [the landlord] wouldn't fix it, so I didn't want to pay rent and then he got it condemned. So that's how he got us kicked out and we couldn't get any of our money back.

In the end, Philip's sense was that he had been swindled and, ultimately, he had to learn a difficult lesson about property contracts and sound financial advice. Shorty after losing the trailer, Philip lost his job at an aluminum factory and because Philip and Ashley's savings had been poured into trying to buy the trailer, they were forced to live on the streets.

Another example of how one participant lost his housing came from Joe. Joe recalled his family's situation from a year ago:

> We lived in The [Shore] for a while and my daughter was raped out there and then the guy who did it and his girlfriend jumped my wife when she confronted them and there was a big fight. I got involved, so well, we were just trying to defend ourselves, but we got blamed because my wife started the confrontation and we got put out. We finally got ourselves another place in Murphysboro. And then, I guess it was about two months ago, it burnt down. The next day I lost my job because the [college] students left [for summer break] and I drove for Yellow Taxi. So, I got laid off and things just went downhill from there. I'm a mechanic. I've built three cars from the ground up. People would bring their cars out to me and stuff, but when we lost our place and I lost my job, I ended up having to sell all my tools and lost everything.

Joe's situation reads like a man trapped in quicksand: the more he struggled to get his finances in order, the worse his situation became. He sold his tools to pay some bills, but now that he had no tools, he had no way of bringing in new income. Without income, he cannot buy new tools and therefore, remained unemployable. He was literally stuck in the vicious cycle. Fortunately, Joe's wife and three children were living with his wife's parents at the time this interview took place. Joe said, "being away from my wife and kids is the most challenging part of [being homeless]," but that he cannot live with them right now because Joe and his wife's father "can't be in the same room together." As evidenced by both Joe's story and Philip's story, the relationship between job security and housing security are closely related when people have no savings, no line of credit, a break in employment, and/or little financial literacy. Given the right set of inopportune circumstances, even a minor setback in financial stability can push someone out of their home.

To be sure, the struggles surrounding financial stability with some participants were more complicated than mere job openings. Five of the participants admitted to having a criminal record that involved jail time and three of those five participants had recently been released from prison and paroled to a homeless shelter because they did not have anywhere else to go. For all three of these participants, this was the first time they had been homeless. According to Brandon:

> Well, this is the first year I've actually ever been in a shelter. I was locked up in the joint and I didn't have any place to parole to in Illinois, so they paroled me to The Lighthouse Shelter in January.... I stayed my time there until April, May; something

like that. And then I came here. I stayed my time here. I think two months ... and then I went to a shelter in Herrin and stayed there for two months. Then my time was up there, so I had to come back here.

Rather surprisingly, "the state knew that [Brandon] was going to the homeless shelter, but it was the only place [he] had to go. The prison officials even gave [him] a ride there." Brandon's story exemplifies the complicated relationship that exists between the criminal justice system and homelessness. Of course, when a criminal has done his or her time, he or she should be released from prison. However, when a person is released into a financially unstable environment, the person has few resources that will enable him or her to make better decisions that lead toward financial stability. This is by no means the fault or responsibility of individual police officers, parole board members, or independent prisons. However, if U.S. American society is serious about addressing the issue of homelessness, then the parole process for criminals with no residence is a factor that ought to be seriously debated.

Unlike Brandon, Michael had a place he might have been able to stay at once he got out of jail (he was currently out on bond), but he was too ashamed to ask. As he told it:

I'm pretty certain that I could have stayed with [one of my buddies] if I had to, but he's got two kids and the stress that would put on him is probably too much. And he's my best friend and I don't want to do that to him. He already helped bond me out.

Because Michael refused to ask for help, he said:

I ended up where I was unable to have anywhere to stay and so I ended up staying in my truck at night and the city park by day. And I didn't know how to be homeless or how to do it. All I knew is that I didn't have anywhere to go and I didn't want to ask anybody for help anymore.

As evident in Michael's story, not asking for help created excessive burdens and only added to the barriers he needed to overcome to get control of his housing and finances. Even though Michael might have been able to overcome some social burdens by asking for help, his criminal record might still have stood in the way of complete financial stability as criminal records had stood in the way for other participants.

Finding and keeping gainful employment can be hard for any homeless person for a multitude of reasons: lack of access to proper identification, gaps in employment history, and transportation to and from work. For convicts, it is nearly impossible. Interestingly, one of the interviewees, James, "used to work [at Good Sam's] 25 years ago." James was a recent parolee who had spent a few months in jail on a drug charge. He came back to Good Sam's trying to pick up a few shifts at the front desk, but his criminal record stood in the way. So James ended up performing day-labor when he could and worked for money "under the table" so he did not "have to pay taxes on that shit." Unfortunately, day-labor is inconsistent, unreliable, and pays poorly; meaning James will probably remain homeless for the foreseeable future. Much like James, Brandon also considered himself a worker. Brandon stated:

> I had a few jobs. I worked in factories over in Kentucky. My family helped me get that job. I was working in a plastics factory until I found a better job that paid a little bit more. But the main job that I had was traveling with carnivals and working carnivals.

However, Brandon's work history was interrupted in his mid-twenties when he began an extensive streak of breaking and entering. He continued:

> I've been locked up most my life. I've been in and out of prison. Now that I'm out, I went to some of the factories and temp places, but I couldn't get nothing. It's been pretty much a regular thing; looking for a job. Most of the jobs that I've had an interview with or a follow up with have all turned me down because of my background. As soon as I got [to Good Sam's] my roommate [Andy] said I could get a job where he's working down at these apartments—refurnishing apartments and painting apartments. So, I went down there and did an okay job the first day. But when I went and talked to the [boss] the next day and let him know about my situation that "Hey I'm pretty much homeless. I'm staying at Good Sam's homeless shelter and I really need this job because I'm on parole...." And then before I could finish, he said, "What are you on parole for?" And I told him that I was on parole for residential burglary and he just said, "Leave. We need you to leave." And that was that.

Ultimately, Brandon's story pushes against the notion that homeless people are lazy and/or lack job skills. It also contradicts the widely-held belief that anybody can get out of poverty if they are willing to work hard (see Scott & Leonhardt, 2005). Brandon was willing to work hard and could perform the duties. Yet, his criminal history made employers leery. As a result, he was left without a job and no job prospects.

To be sure, Brandon is responsible for his crimes and he should have to deal with the consequences. However, it is also undeniable that his criminal history had immediate and long-term consequences for his community, whether the community wants to deal with the consequences or not. On a larger scale, the reality is that unless Brandon (and others like him) can find gainful employment, his condition remains a public burden: he will continue to live on the streets or in a shelter, collect food stamps, and require public resources for basic necessities. While avoiding hiring people with criminal histories may be rational in the short-term for employers, it is not a long-term solution for creating a community where all citizens contribute to the community's economic well-being. Therefore, it would be advantageous for communities to engage with employers in determining how to help former convicts like Brandon gain financial independence or risk the long-term consequences of Brandon's public dependency.

Loss of Physical Health, Safety, and Material Possessions

In addition to discussing their dire financial situations, participants also talked about the devastating physical impact that homelessness can assert on one's body and personal possessions. Notably, some participants struggled physically before they became homeless, but uncomfortable living situations and restricted access to medications exacerbated their problems. For example, Malcolm had been paroled to Good Sam's in early June 2013 after spending a few months in county jail. While in jail he was on a daily regimen of methadone to help ease withdrawal symptoms associated with heroin. Now that he was out of jail and no longer had access to this medication, he became lethargic, confused, and constantly had to carry a roll of paper towels to control his continual drooling. Without medication, his only options were to fight through the withdrawal symptoms until they subsided or start using heroin to balance his system. Malcolm would choose to fight through the symptoms, but it took nearly two months before his body returned to a state of normalcy.

While Malcolm's physical ailments were acquired through drug use and withdrawal, others experienced painful physical conditions as a direct result of being homeless. The most common conditions people complained about included: lack of sleep from sleeping in strange places; sore legs and feet from walking everywhere; skin rashes and diseases from having close contact with people who did not wash themselves or their clothes frequently; and back pain. As reported by the participants, back pain was the result of awkward sleeping situations. This included sleeping on uneven ground, sleeping on concrete, sleeping in tight spaces (such as a crate for safety), sleeping on inadequate mattresses, and sleeping in vehicles. As Michael recalled:

> The biggest challenge for me was not having something to lay on and I couldn't lay my body flat in my pickup and that was hurting me. I might have been able do it when I was younger, but [sleeping in my pickup] was hurting me. I aggravated my back. And I went to the hospital and my [X-ray] was covered in white hairs and on an X-ray that's arthritis. And a doctor typed up a letter to me that said that this type of arthritis would have been aggressive for even somebody twice my age.

Michael's back problems prohibited him from performing manual labor for more than a couple of hours a day, which limited his ability to find a full-time job. In order to dull the pain, Michael was "tempted to get an ounce of cocaine to help the pain," but chose not to because he was "tired of living in [his] criminal past."

Uncomfortable living conditions are not the only threat impacting a homeless person's physical well-being. In short, homeless people are also confronted with physical assaults that range from mocking gestures to violent beatings. While all forms of physical assaults are deplorable, some of the less threatening instances involved drivers throwing items out of car windows. For example, Kenneth said:

> I've had some people throw food at me or throw coins at me. Not a hand full of coins or nothing like that, but like I had a guy a couple of days ago that just threw out a penny; like he just tried to hit me with it.

Joe experienced similar situations and recalled having cheeseburgers, bottles of water, and ice cream thrown at him while standing at an intersection, near a McDonald's, asking people for spare change. In a rather detached tone, Joe stated that, "I think they buy a little extra just to throw it at me."

For Kenneth and Joe, these types of acts are dehumanizing at worst, but neither participant felt unsafe during the violent exchange. However, two female participants did express feelings of fear during confrontations with sexually-aggressive men. For instance, Ashley said that while she was standing on the corner asking drivers for spare change:

> I had one guy spit at me. Yeah, it was a man and I standing over here while he drove by a couple of times; which is scary anytime a guy keeps driving back and forth staring at you. Finally, he rolled down his window and asked, "How much for oral sex?" You

know, I won't say the exact words he used, but I said, "I'm not out here for that," because I'm not.... And he said, "Well, you're a bitch ass ho anyway" and spit at me as he drove off. I thought he might circle back again as he was doing all day to harass me some more, so I just ran to my husband crying because I was scared and that was really uncalled for. You don't have to like me or read my sign, but if you read it, don't look down on me like some ho on the corner. If you don't like [my sign], then you don't have to read it. You can just go on and leave me alone.

Kristen had a similar story of being targeted by a man that "kept stalking me until he got me someplace where we were alone. Fortunately a waiter came out the back door [into an alley] for a smoke break and the guy ran off." Kristen's and Ashley's stories are reminiscent of the unwanted sexualized role women are sometimes placed in while they are homeless (see Huey & Berndt, 2008). With their bodies on public display, Kristen and Ashley were vulnerable to objectifying comments as well as physical intimidation. Unfortunately, Ashley, specifically, was stuck in a conundrum; she could remove herself from the public's eye and risk losing public assistance, or she could stay in the public's eye and risk further confrontation. Because Ashley was standing on the corner "to support [her] daughter," Ashley vowed to be "out here today, tomorrow, next week, next month; as long as it takes to get [her daughter] into an apartment."

Besides confronting the physical challenges that affect the body's health and sense of safety, interviewees also faced physical challenges with regard to their personal possessions. Because few homeless people have anywhere to store their personal possessions, they must always travel with everything they own or hide their belongings in public places such as dumpsters, bushes, or drainage pipes. Kenneth chose to carry everything he owned and "travel light. Otherwise people will get at your stuff." As illustration, Kenneth told me that he knew another homeless person who:

... had a bunch of stuff in a cart that he kept behind Wal-Mart and he stashed it where he thought it wouldn't be bothered. But when he went to get it last month it was gone. It wasn't much for someone like you, but that was everything he had: a suitcase with clean clothes, a radio, a couple of books, and some things that other people had given him to hold onto. It all just came up missing.

The occasional stressing over one's personal possessions is an emotion to which many housed people can probably relate. However, during this research, it seemed as if property protection was a constant battle for the homeless. For example, Philip recalled leaving his bike in front of McDonald's while he ran in to get a soda for "no more than two minutes." When he returned, "somebody had stolen [his] bike." Philip was particularly upset about this incident:

> My sign was still leaning there against the pole. It's clear that I got a sign and some other stuff laying there next to the bike. I'm already down. Whoever did this could have read the sign next to the bike and knew I was homeless. How much more you got to kick me? I couldn't have had that bike much more than 24-hours before somebody's got to steal it. That's two bikes I've lost in two weeks.

In a similar vein, Tiffany stated that she was "always worrying about not knowing if my stuff is going to be [where I left it] or if it's going to be safe." She did mention that this was not always the case and that when she first became homeless she did not worry about people stealing her personal possessions because "who would want a bunch of homeless person's junk?" However, her vigilance increased after the summer of 2012:

> My stuff was at the Econo Lodge storage bin and I went back to check on it and somebody went through all my stuff and it's all over the floor. So I don't even know what's missing and what's not. And I can't really do anything about it. I don't have anywhere to take it or anyway to transport it anywhere. So I just had to leave it all and walk away. What else am I supposed to do? So, yeah, it's hard because that's all we had.

In each of these stories about personal possessions, there are themes of stress, endless worry, nervousness, and constant vigilance. More than personal property is the identification with this property as "all they have." Therefore, when someone steals, damages, or flippantly disregards their items as trash, homeless people have reason to take it personally. In witnessing their only possessions being treated with such disrespect, homeless people feel fully disrespected and disregarded as human beings. In short, they too, are made to feel like trash.

Loss of Family

Tragically, homeless people oftentimes lose something far more valuable than physical health, safety, or material possessions. They lose family. For a variety of reasons, familial relationships become strained while a person is homeless. According to the participants, the major reason is money. Of the ten people interviewed, eight mentioned that they had lived with a family member and/or borrowed money from a family member immediately prior to becoming homeless. During somewhere between six months and two years of dependency, six of these relationships would become stressed and the housed family member would ask the interviewee to leave and/or cut him or her off financially. Unfortunately, this type of ending usually meant that long-term damage had been caused to the relationship and many of the participants now struggled to reconcile with their loved ones.

This is what happened to Michael's relationship with his father as Michael relied on his dad's finances to help him fight criminal charges. Michael said:

> At first, I was unable to accept that this had happened to me; that I had to fight a cocaine charge and a rape charge at the same time. The cocaine charge would have been just probation because it was my first offense, but now that I got a rape charge, I could be facing twenty years. What people think from my town is that I'm fine because my folks are helping me [financially]. People in town know that my folks aren't wealthy, but they also know that my folks have put a lot of money into lawyers. They keep up with my folks and they know that we've got about $20,000 in a lawyer. They know that [my folks] paid this recent $5,000 bond. They probably think that I'm fine, but the truth is, is that this has gave my dad a mental fit. He's losing his mind over losing that kind of money. And he's getting ready to take more money out of his retirement for my lawyer. That's a lot of money for him. Did he have it? Yeah. But he didn't have it to let go of for nothing. And that's really what it's come down to. Him losing it over nothing.

During this portion of the interview, Michael was visibly distraught over the entire situation. Yet, his stress had little to do with his pending legal situation. In fact, Michael seemed at peace with his pending twenty-year prison sentence. Instead, the only thing Michael seemed truly concerned with was helping his dad and mending their relationship. While he admitted to using and dealing cocaine, he denied that he ever raped anyone. However, Michael did say:

> My criminal life finally just caught up with me. Whether I raped anyone or not, I kind of deserve this. But my dad, he doesn't deserve any of this. I think about him having to go through this and it's really uncalled for. I just think about how I upended his life overnight. I just want to go back to how things were with my old house and my old job. I'm well aware that I'll never be able to pay my dad back twenty, twenty-five, thirty thousand dollars—whatever it ends up being. But I just want to make the effort and try to make this right before he dies so that he can have a retirement and we can get back on good terms.

Like Michael, several participants mentioned the sentiment of "making an effort" to reconcile broken family relationships. Besides finances,

94

participants mentioned prior drug use, alcohol use, and violence as reasons their families had chosen to break ties. Unsurprisingly, not a single participant blamed family members for the broken relationships and instead, each participant took full responsibility. However, as Kristen talked about healing these relationships, she mentioned that "the difficult part is just convincing your family that you've changed now even though you've dragged them through this shit 15 other times."

Certainly, there were times when fragmented family relationships were more directly caused by outside circumstances rather than intrafamilial tensions. In the cases of Brandon, Maddy, Ashley, and Philip, their family units were actively striving to remain intact, but legal systems were keeping them apart. For Brandon, being away from his family:

> was emotionally hard. It bothered me that I couldn't go home. I couldn't parole over with my family in Kentucky because I got misdemeanor warrants and fines over there. So, yeah, it kind of bothers me. I wish I could be over there with my family, but I can't until I can get me a job and pay off those fines. I got misdemeanor warrants and fines that need to get paid so I don't get locked up. I'm hoping that [Illinois will let me parole in Kentucky] because my sister's gonna write up a letter saying that they'll allow me to stay with them and that they got a job ready for me. So I'd get an interstate compact and go ahead and parole over [in Kentucky] so I can see my family while I'm working off the fines. So maybe [Kentucky] will be lenient on me and won't lock me up if I'm working to pay [the fines]. That's what I'm hoping, but I have my doubts.

In Brandon's case, he was trying to challenge two state criminal justice systems at once. He wanted to leave Illinois to live with his family in Kentucky, but Illinois was prohibiting him from leaving Illinois while he was on parole. Additionally, Brandon was trying to get work in Kentucky to pay legal fines to Kentucky, but if he stepped foot in Kentucky, Kentucky would arrest him for outstanding warrants. For any person caught in the chaos of homelessness, it seems logical that a steady job and family support would help create the necessary conditions for stability and recovery. However, because his family lived outside his parole boundaries, Brandon was legally prohibited from utilizing the strength and resources of his family relationships, such as emotional support, housing, and job placement. By not being able to utilize these family resources, Brandon was forced to continue wandering southern Illinois from one homeless shelter to the next every 30 days with no direction, no job prospects, and no emotional support.

Perhaps the most heartbreaking incidences of broken families involved homeless people who were currently separated from their children. For example, Maddy was a 30-year-old mother who had a 15-year-old child. Living an unstable financial life was something Maddy had become accustomed to over the years since she had grown up poor and "had pretty much been on [her] own [her] whole life." Maddy also mentioned that "Hell, the first time my mom kicked me out was when I was nine." Therefore, living her life in and out of homelessness no longer took the "emotional toll that it probably takes on other people." However, Maddy did express strong emotions when speaking about her daughter, whom she had not seen in over six months. Explaining the reasons for their separation, Maddy said:

> I'm originally from up north [Illinois]. I moved around a bit after my daughter was born; with her father—to Missouri—but her father never really wanted anything to do with us so we moved backed in with my mom so I could finish high school. A few years ago, I followed some friends to Iowa. It wasn't much; just waitressing, but I had to get out of here. Well, that didn't last long because when my daughter was 13 she got raped by a friend of ours. I was stupid and reported it and when the cops found out that we didn't have much, the state said that [my daughter] was living in an "unfit environment." Anyway [Department of Children and Family Services] took her and I'm working to get her back. So, I moved back [to Illinois] because I have a better chance of making a stable life here opposed to Iowa. Hopefully, I'll have her back here around November once DCFS sees that I have a job and proper housing.

In Maddy's case, she was faced with trying to understand a difficult paradox: do not report a rape and keep her daughter or report a rape and lose her daughter. For a person who is homeless, dealing with state resources, specifically the Department of Children and Family Services, can be a delicate process that sometimes involves half-truths and strategic omissions in an effort to get help while keeping the family intact. In fact, the uncertainty that comes with accepting public assistance is one of the reasons some homeless families simply avoid state assistance in the first place (Williams, 2003). On the one hand, people who are homeless want assistance for their family. On the other hand, people who are homeless do not want to be seen as unfit parents and risk losing their children. Unfortunately, the lesson Maddy learned was to not ask for help in the future because if she had known that the state was going to take her daughter, she "would have never reported [the rape]."

Like Maddy, Philip and Ashley were in a similar struggle with the

Department of Children and Family Services regarding their four-year-old daughter. When I first met this married couple in July, Ashley had told me that her "daughter usually stays with her cousin a couple days a week so that [Philip and I] can work together out here and my husband can go fill out applications." At the end of the day, it was expected that Ashley's cousin would drop off Ashley's daughter and this remained the routine until the beginning of August. During the first week of August, I was out collecting data when Philip approached with a panicked look on his face. Apparently, Ashley had gotten into a fight with her cousin:

> [Her cousin] got mad and she wouldn't bring the baby back. I said, "Why don't you bring the baby back?" She said, "No, I got something for you. I'm not going to bring the baby back." And the next thing you know she called DCFS and said that I sexually assaulted my kid and physically beat her. Anyway, [DCFS] came and they took the baby. And [DCFS] checked up on [the abuse allegations] and none of that was true or nothing, but then the allegations against me is that [DCFS] don't feel like [my daughter's] in a stable environment because we don't have housing and we live day by day at the hotel and stuff. And the woman says, "Who knows when you all will be put out or something like that?" I even had the hotel vouch for me. I've never missed a payment when I've had my daughter with me. I mean, I've slept on the streets. But she's never slept on the streets. Not when she's with me.

Philip and Ashley lost their daughter because of the subjective conclusions of a DCFS social worker. Now that their homeless status was known, getting their daughter back was going to be a lengthy process. According to Philip, they had to first move into an apartment and then prove that they had a steady income before the state would return their daughter. However, Philip had been filling out job applications for the past several months with no luck. With no job prospects, this was proving to be a near impossible task. Most difficult for Philip was that he did not know where his daughter was. As he relayed:

> [DCFS] won't tell us where she is. They said something about foster care, but I'm trying to get one of my family members or one of [Ashley's] family members to get her out. I want to know where my kid is, but our next official court date isn't until October. Like I said, none of this was proven. There were no physical signs of abuse, you know. How can you just take somebody's kid based on what somebody said that turns out false?

Talking with Philip that day was incredibly difficult. He had found himself in an impossible position where he had lost his daughter and had no way of reaching out to her except through the lengthy court process. Furthermore, with no housing and no job, it was a real possibility that he and his wife would not regain custody for the foreseeable future. Knowing that housing and a job were essential in his fight, Philip asked me, "You still got my number? It's 618-[number withheld]. If you know of anybody's who's got a job, please, please, please give me a call. I gotta get my kid back." Sadly, what remained unknown during our conversation was how his four-year-old daughter was handling the transition. According to Philip, he had "been with her her whole life." Therefore, not only were the parents going through emotional turmoil during this ordeal, but it was quite possible that their four-year-old daughter was scared, anxious, and/or confused about being placed into the foster care system with strangers. Quite possibly, she was also asking a DCFS social worker about where her family was in an effort to reunite with her parents.

Loss of Self

The totality of this accumulating loss wore on all of the participants and ultimately caused each one of them to (at least partially) lose their sense of self. No longer could they find their identity in their professions, their possessions, or their families. In short, each participant's life had spiraled so far out of control that the participant had a hard time articulating who exactly he or she was anymore. In order to make it through each day, Tiffany said, "You got to be strong to handle it out here. If you're not strong, you're not going to handle it. To live outside is hard. People just got to stay strong or they'll lose their mind." Unfortunately, Tiffany's advice was easier said than done. In the following passage, Michael captures why being homeless was emotionally difficult for him. He said:

> It's a real mental challenge for me. It's like, I haven't been unemployed for like 11 years and I've always had insurance. Now I'm a part of the system that I want nothing to do with. Having to get food stamps and asking people for help. I don't have insurance. It's degrading. You know, I'm lucky though because I haven't come across many people from back home. So they don't really know what's going on.

At the age of 37, Michael was experiencing homelessness for the first time. Now that he was homeless, he wanted to keep it a secret from as many friends and family members as he could. Being homeless had become a point of shame for Michael and he did not want others to identify him as a homeless person who had become dependent on government welfare and/or charity. However, he could not hide this reality from himself and was forced to confront the fact that he no longer had financial stability. In turn, his sense of self was shifting from a financially-independent housed person to a welfare-receiving homeless person. The fact that Michael was homeless and dependent on the finances of others "hurt [his] pride" and made him think about "how [he] ended up here." Therefore, one of the ways to help a person like Michael regain his sense of self is by helping him transition from a state of dependency to a state of independence (Murray, 2012).

Another participant who talked about how homelessness affected her pride was Ashley. Ashley "had worked from the age of 16 to the age of 32" until she became disabled. While standing out in the sun all day asking for change, Ashley said:

> I don't want to be out here. This is embarrassing. You know, I'm burnt to a crisp out here. I'd much rather be working eight-hour days inside, but I can't. I got some of my husband's family around here that's always asking, "Why would you do this?" But I guess you never know what you'd do until you're in this situation. I mean, I used to work, but now I'm disabled. And public aid doesn't help that much. So I have to be out here all burnt up in the sun. And for me to stand out here and swallow my pride is a big thing because I've worked and I've never had to beg, but here I am, you know. But I got a kid to take care of, so I have to swallow it.

Throughout the interviews, "embarrassment" was a common word used by participants to describe how they felt about their public image. Furthermore, all of the participants were well aware of the public stigma associated with being homeless. In an act of resistance against this stigma, Kristen went so far as to confront me during the interview and abrasively shouted:

> You think I like being like this?! I hate it! It's embarrassing! People are always doing bad things to me! I don't know what to do. I hate everybody! When you're out like this, people want to rub it in your face like it's funny. It's not funny! I know a bunch of friends who've died this year! I'm afraid that I'm going to die!

Kristen's words moved from accusatory to agony; her tone started off angry, but almost immediately became desperate. At the end of this outburst, Kristen buried her face in her hands and leaned over in exhaustion. As she gathered her belongings and walked away from the interview, Kristen wanted reassurance that she would make it through her bout with homelessness. She wanted an answer as to "when [she was] going to find [herself] again." Interestingly, her phrasing detached the idea of "homelessness" from her identity. This phrasing was common for other participants as well. In other words, some homeless people would not accept the idea that their true self was a homeless person. Instead, they talked about how they were "searching" for their true self like it was some sort of journey.

In addition to dealing with the abstract concepts of embarrassment, pride, and sense of self, participants also confronted more concrete concerns, such as the endless worry over daily necessities. According to Ashley, "You wake up every morning and you constantly worry, 'Am I going to be able to get through the day?' Cuz you never know. You might not." In Kenneth's case, his constant worry over daily necessities sometimes led to depression. He stated:

> I get depressed a lot, especially if I don't get a good few nights of sleep or some food or money. If you don't get any money, you can't stay at a hotel. If you get money, but no food, you can pay for a hotel, but you might have to go to bed hungry. If you don't get neither, then you have to go to bed hungry and it's not going to be in a hotel. It's just worrying all the time. I never know what's going to happen.

Later Kenneth said, "the biggest challenge is just being out here all the time and having to deal with not having a place to stay all the time. It can definitely be emotionally and mentally challenging." Kenneth's statements highlight one of the many divides between the homeless and the housed community. Whereas many housed people may take food and shelter for granted, homeless people are forced to struggle for these resources every day. Having to constantly struggle for food and shelter leaves homeless people with little time for managing other aspects of life, such as family, education, résumé-building, or personal care. Consequently, while homeless people are stuck fighting for survival in the short-term, they are prohibited from working on items that may help them in the long-term. In the end, worrying about food and shelter makes it nearly impossible to better one's education and job skills. Thus, people without basic necessities fall further and further behind.

For some participants, the continuous worry over basic needs, such as food and shelter, not only caused personal anxiety, but was also a source of violent outburst. As Tiffany said:

> It makes you want to get violent. Your anxiety level goes up. It just does. You can blow up at the drop of a hat. And people do. People argue a lot around here. We try

100

not to, but you can't help it. Sometimes it gets physically violent and then you realize it's over stupid shit like cleaning a table or borrowing a towel. Hell, people be fighting over free stuff. How stupid is that?

In time, these verbal and physical outbursts can cause rifts within the homeless community. During observations at the shelter, it was clear that small cliques of four to six people had formed based on an altercation that had happened in May 2013. When asked what had happened, one of the residents stated that "a pushing match had started between [Mia and Tina] over some shoes from the church van." Two months later, people were still angry about the situation and this created unhealthy emotional tension and stress within the community.

Indeed, expressions of violence toward others were not the only ways participants processed their situation. Quite overwhelmingly, nine of the participants talked openly about "crying every day" and six mentioned thoughts of suicide. Philip's remarks captured these sentiments most profoundly and are worth quoting at length. Philip, a 49-year-old husband and father to a four-year-old, said:

Shoot, I cry all the time. I mean, I'm a man, but I cry all the time. I cry for the simple fact that I'm a man and that a man should be able to provide more for his family, you know. So, I cry for all this. I mean, I have strength—it takes a lot of mental strength to be out here trying to be that man that I should be. But then I look at it and at least I'm a man that's still sticking around. Because, well, I'm a black man and I know a lot of black men who have kids who don't give a crap about them. I'm just saying in general. I'm from the 'hood. I grew up in the 'hood and you got babies strung up everywhere and ain't no men to take care of them. They're not even trying! Hell, I know some men who got jobs and don't even try to help they kids out. So, I look at it like "I don't even have a job, but I'm actually there for my baby!" And that gives me motivation to come out here another day. That gives me motivation to not go out and bust a car window and steal a radio for quick cash because I know I want to be there for my daughter. I want to be there for her and for her to get an education and for her to possibly grow up and have a life; a better life than I got. So, yeah, I cry. But I'd rather be crying trying to make something for my daughter than hanging out somewhere having a good time and her never know who her daddy is.

Like Philip, many participants cried for the want of a better life, either for themselves or for their loved ones. Michael cried because his criminal history and lawyer fees had fractured his relationship with his father. Tiffany cried because she witnessed her 22-year-old son fall into homelessness alongside her. Kristen cried because she felt alone. And Maddy cried because "this wasn't the life [she] had imagined for [herself]."

These moments of intense sadness and disappointment led some participants to think about suicide. As Philip continued:

> Sometimes I just want to stand out there and walk in front of a truck because I get so depressed. And especially when there ain't no money coming in and the hotel where we're staying is like, "You have to have money today or we're throwing you out!" And we've been thrown out before. So they're not joking. It's not easy—mentally. People probably think that it's so easy for you to stand out here and get money from other people, but it's not as easy as it looks. It's hard. Trust me; it'd be a whole lot easier for me to throw myself in front of that truck right now. And if you catch me on a bad day, I just might.

While Philip mentioned that he "couldn't commit suicide right now" because he had a wife and daughter to take care of, there was one particular participant who spoke as if he had nothing keeping him from killing himself. As he discussed his feelings, Joe said:

> Hell, I was in shock for a while. Now I'm just numb. I don't know what to feel. I don't know what to think. Before, I was a little scared. I didn't know what was going to happen or where I was going to go. I used to cry, but now it's straight numbness. It's always like that now. Hell, I'm not even bothered about being homeless now. So, what's the point?

Joe seemed to have lost hope about his situation improving. Whereas others were still fighting for their dignity, Joe had grown tired of being homeless for the past year. Moreover, since Joe's wife and children were being taken care of by his wife's parents, Joe was "not sure that moving back in with [him] is their best option." Slowly, Joe seemed to be convincing himself that his family's life would improve if he just committed suicide.

6. Navigating the System

During the summer of 2013, I sometimes had to work a graveyard shift at Good Sam's. The graveyard shift ran from midnight to 8:00 a.m. and mostly required me to do paperwork, cleaning, laundry, and make breakfast. Overall, this was a relatively quiet shift until people began waking up around 6:00 a.m. On one particular Saturday morning in late July, a single mom, Becky, marched her four young children out into the common area and began pouring them cereal. The children were relatively well-behaved and smiling and laughing with one another while their mother got breakfast ready. Abruptly, their playfulness was interrupted by their mother's violent temper. "Everyone knock it off and be quiet!" she yelled. She then ordered the oldest, 10-year-old Max, to take his siblings to the table closest to the television set and to turn on *SpongeBob SquarePants*. Max dutifully complied, carrying 9-month-old Amanda while 7-year-old Jo and 5-year-old Sam followed. A few moments later, Becky delivered three bowls of puffed rice cereal and a warmed bottle for little Amanda and said, "Now you kids sit here and eat!" Jo tried to protest and with her head hung low, she mumbled, "But I don't like this cereal." Becky quickly grabbed Jo by the checks and turned Jo's head so that the two of them made eye-contact. "I don't care what you want. These bowls better be empty." Becky pushed Jo's face away from her and then made eye-contact with Max and Sam. "And if I hear that any of you were acting up while I was gone, you're all going to get it."

Becky then left the building and spent the next hour smoking cigarettes at the picnic table out back. The longer she was gone, the more furious I became with her behavior. First, it looked that her children were well-behaved and did not warrant the type of public lashing she had given them so early in the morning. Second, it seemed wholly inappropriate of her to leave her four young children alone in the common area of a homeless shelter while strangers wandered in and out of the shelter all morning. As a staff member, it was my responsibility to confront her about her irresponsible behavior, and as a researcher, it was of interest to figure out why she had engaged in this type of behavior.

When the situation had calmed down enough to approach Becky, I walked outside and simply asked, "What do you have going on today?" Distraught and exhausted, Becky quietly remarked, "Everything." She continued:

> I have two interviews on the other side of town. [Jo's] had a rash now for about a week and I need to finally get her to a doctor. And [Max's] dad keeps calling me about visitation. He's supposed to be with his dad on the weekends, but I don't have any way to get him over there. Plus, I'm supposed to take this test today in Marion, but I can't get all the way over to Marion and back so I'll probably just miss it and that'll set me back another month until they offer [the test] again.

The short conversation with Becky was enlightening and forced me to reconsider the judgmental attitude that had overshadowed the previous hour. This is not to say that her callous behavior suddenly warranted approval. However, there was now a better understanding of where her callousness was coming from and a sobering amount of empathy for her situation.

It warrants mentioning Marion is a 17-mile drive from Carbondale. In a personal vehicle, it is about a 25-minute trip (one-way). However, many people without personal vehicles have to use a shuttle service between Carbondale and Marion. This trip can take over an hour (one-way) due to stops and pick-ups along the way.

Becky's day was full, chaotic, and uncertain. To top it off, she was living in a homeless shelter with her four kids, no job, and no idea where she was going to go once her 30-day stay was up. Without a car, no employment, little money, and four children, the pressure of her situation was simply overwhelming.

Reflecting on Riis's (1890) *How the Other Half Lives*, it is sensible to think about how ordered most people's lives are when compared to the uncertainty that oftentimes accompanies homeless people while they are navigating the culture of homelessness. For example, most people know when they have to work, when they get paid, where they can get food, and where they were going to sleep at night. Most people also know that if they get sick, they can immediately visit the doctor.

104

However, because the homeless lack basic necessities (Miller, et al., 2004), they must constantly secure food and shelter in a system that Kenneth described as "different every day. I don't think there's no such things as a usual day. I just don't know what I'll eat or when or if things will pick back up. I'm hoping I'll be inside tonight, but you never know." Having to constantly navigate a system in search of basic necessities leaves homeless people little time to further their education, develop job skills, or find stable income. Building upon these ideas, this chapter will illustrate how homeless people navigate the culture of homelessness as well as explain how homeless people secure basic goods, utilize public services, and look for steady income. In organizing this chapter, first, it will discuss how homeless people navigate living on the streets. Second, it analyzes how homeless people work their way through the shelter system. Third, it looks at the different ways homeless people attempt to get jobs. Next, it talks about how the homeless rely on the charity of others. Finally, it moves through the process of obtaining government assistance, such as housing vouchers, unemployment insurance, disability insurance, and food stamps.

Navigating the Streets

When initially talking with people who slept on the streets, the immediate thought was to ask them, "Why don't you just sleep at Good Sam's?" At first, this question seemed innocuous. In all, it was understandable why some people might avoid hanging around the shelter during the day: fear of being noticed, dislike for other residents, or looking for work. But at night, a bed and a roof seemed like a better alternative compared to all of the sleeping conditions witnessed on the street during the course of this research. Yet, after learning about the experiences of some participants, it was realized that the answers to the aforementioned question were oftentimes far more complicated than one could have imagined.

When discussing this issue with Joe, Joe casually said that he slept on the streets because Kenneth preferred to sleep on the streets. "[Kenneth] and I are brothers," Joe would repeatedly say throughout the interview. And while not biologically related, Joe said that the two had known each other all their lives and that Joe would do anything for

Kenneth. When Joe was asked why Kenneth preferred to sleep on the streets, Joe answered:

> I don't really know. I just know that he doesn't like [Good Sam's].... He's never really said much about Good Sam's. He just doesn't talk much about it. He just really don't like being there, so we stay out here. I mean, he really don't like being out here either, but what other choice do we have?

Two weeks after speaking with Joe, Kenneth was interviewed and pressed on this same issue. After dodging initial request, Kenneth said:

> I used to use Good Sam's a lot, but I've been over there so much in the last few years and I just don't think they want me back anymore. That's really the only resource I know. They might let me get lunch and dinner, but I've stayed there too many times already. I just can't stay there anymore.

From these remarks, it sounded like Kenneth felt as if he had overstayed his welcome at Good Sam's. While it was not clear whether Kenneth was asked to leave by the staff, or whether he felt coerced out for other reasons, his remarks do suggest that there was some type of falling out between Kenneth and the shelter staff. Upon further exploration as to why some homeless people no longer felt welcomed at Good Sam's, there emerged two possible answers.

First, as part of a larger policy, Good Sam's does have an extensive "Banned List" of people who are no longer allowed to stay at the shelter due to previous violations including violence, possession of weapons, possession of drugs, and threatening behavior. Depending on the severity of the violation, people can be placed on the "Banned List" anywhere from six months to life. While it is not suggested that Kenneth necessarily falls into this category, it is concluded that the "Banned List" does provide at least one answer as to why some homeless people live on the streets instead of staying at the shelter.

The second possible reason people might avoid the shelter is the issue of safety (see Ravenhill, 2008; see Walsh, 1992). As highlighted in Chapter 5, interpersonal relationships among homeless people can become abrasive, threatening, and even violent. Consequently, if a homeless person feels threatened by other members of the homeless community he or she may simply choose to sleep on the streets as opposed to staying at a shelter and risk coming face-to-face with confrontation. Therefore, it is plausible that when Kenneth mentioned that "they" do not want him back at Good Sam's, he might have been talking about other patrons with whom he wanted to avoid confrontation.

Whatever the specific reason, Kenneth no longer felt welcomed at Good Sam's and since Good Sam's is the only shelter in town, he was compelled to sleep on the streets in the company of his loyal friend Joe.

Aside from those participants who were forced to sleep on the streets through a banned list or interpersonal intimidation, there were also participants who simply preferred sleeping outside. For example, Tiffany and her husband occasionally chose to live in the woods because they wanted a type of privacy that the shelter did not afford. Tiffany explained that in the woods, "We have our privacy when we live in the tents. We have our own little spot to go to when it gets hectic [in the shelter]. Nobody knows where it is. It's nice and clean and secluded." When asked about how she initially discovered her home in the woods, Tiffany said:

> To find a spot, you have to walk around for a long time and just look for a spot. When we found our spot, we called the police department and asked if it was okay that we stayed there 'cause there were no "No Trespassing" signs or anything like that. So [the police] said we were fine. You just have to walk around and look.

I was rather taken aback by the thought of Tiffany asking the police for permission to set up residence in the city's woods and she elaborated with:

> Yep, the police, Sergeant [Baker] said: "Out of sight, out of mind." Just as long as the public doesn't see your tent and as long as property owners, you know business owners, don't mind. We have like three or four business owners in front of us that we can see from the woods, but they all said that [they are] okay with [us staying there] because we keep it clean and don't make any noise.

Like Tiffany, James also sometimes chose to live outside because of how crowded and public the shelter became. At the time of our interview, James was sleeping in an alley between two businesses that had "a little porch over it that's holding up [his] roof." He was coming to Good Sam's during the day to take a shower and eat. I visited his sleeping quarters a few days after the interview and discovered that the roof he had spoken about consisted of layered cardboard that he had tied to the metal piping and metal fire escape that ran just overhead. During the interview, James admitted that the outdoor shelter he had created for himself was not as safe as staying at Good Sam's, "but it [kept] the rain out." Additionally, James was vigilant about his safety. For instance, he mentioned that the summer was the best time to sleep outside because of how active people were at night; specifically around the bars and late-night restaurants. Sometimes James said, "I feel vulnerable as far as somebody trying to come up and hurt me or whatever. But as long as I sleep in well-lit areas where I know people will be hanging around businesses at night, I feel pretty safe."

In addition to safety, participants who lived outside also mentioned other challenges such as the weather and personal hygiene. Whereas James stayed within walking distance of Good Sam's so that he could frequently use their shower, restroom, and shelter from extreme heat or extreme cold, this was not the case for all participants. For example, Joe would have liked to use Good Sam's daytime resources more often, but "getting around is hard because the only way [he] can get around is by foot." Therefore, when those who lack transportation need shelter from the weather or need to use the restroom, they are oftentimes at the mercy of local businesses. Unfortunately, not all businesses are hospitable to these needs.

On one particularly hot day in June 2013, Tiffany and her husband tried to cool off by sitting in a local restaurant. Since the restaurant was mostly empty, Tiffany did not think it would be a problem for them to rest in the air conditioning for a few minutes. However, as Tiffany recalled:

> Some businesses mind. Some businesses you can't go in unless you're buying something. Some of them don't mind; especially when it's hot. They understand. But, yeah, we were told to leave Pag's. You can't go in there unless you're buying something. They didn't care how hot it was. We only wanted a glass of water for like 10 minutes. Nope. They threw us out and they'll throw you out too unless you pay for something. It's terrible.

Stories about being asked to leave businesses were conveyed by seven different participants and the context by which most of these stories were told was in relation to using the restroom. As previously discussed in Chapter 5, Kenneth was banned from using the restroom in McDonald's because of his bad hygiene. Others told stories about having to buy something before they were allowed to use the restroom. Interestingly enough, these types of restroom restrictions made some participants actively prepare their daily restroom routines. For instance, while having to go to the restroom outside "isn't that big of a deal for guys," said Tiffany, "it's kind of a problem for girls." Therefore, to plan for this problem, Tiffany always makes sure she has enough change in her pockets to buy a cup of coffee just in case she is asked to make a purchase.

Navigating the Shelters

The alternative to living on the streets is attempting to navigate the shelter system. In southern Illinois, the most difficult part of navigating the shelter system is the fact that most community shelters only allow residents to stay up to 30 days. After 30 days are up, a person has the choice of sleeping outside for the next month or traveling to a different town and staying at a different shelter for 30 days. However, this choice is oftentimes dictated by external circumstances. For example, Kristen was a 42-year-old female who was sleeping in her truck during the time of our interview. She had recently been discharged from Good Sam's on July 19, 2013, after her 30-day-limit was reached. She now had to wait 30 days post-discharge to readmit herself. She said, "I would love to be staying indoors right now, but I've been living right out there in my truck for the past two weeks because I can't come in [to Good Sam's] until [August] nineteenth." When asked why she did not just drive to Marion and stay at a nearby shelter, which also followed the "30 days stay/30 days wait for readmission" model, Kristen replied:

> I don't really like going to Marion because it's a hassle getting from here to there. Plus it costs me a lot in gas money. It's just too difficult to travel if I ever have to come back [to Carbondale] for anything. I am trying to find work around here and if they call me for an interview, it's just too much. I'd rather just stay in my truck and wait it out.

For Kristen, who had a rather small build, sleeping in her truck did not pose the type of physical challenges that it might have caused larger people. Additionally, because she parked her truck next to Good Sam's and "under a street light," she felt "perfectly safe." However, she did talk about "how cold it gets out here at night" and that sometimes she wakes up "five or six times a night just shaking." For Kristen, "the nineteenth can't come soon enough."

For those who were able to travel from shelter to shelter every 30 days, there were other barriers that sometimes stood in the way. One of the most egregious barriers discussed was race. On no fewer than seven occasions, people at Good Sam's were observed talking about perceived racial discrimination at a shelter in Marion. More specifically, black male patrons would talk about having "no place to go" once their 30-day-limit was up at Good Sam's because the shelter "don't let blacks stay there." When it was attempted to gather more information about these claims, people's remarks became more measured with statements such as "you can't have a criminal record; period" and "you can't be an addict." However, each of these conversations always ended with a variation of "but they let white people in who have criminal records and are addicts." For example, Tiffany discussed being turned away from the shelter and said:

> The lady turned us away because we're an interracial couple. There was me and my husband and then this other guy and his girlfriend behind us who was an interracial couple. Then there was this white couple behind them. Both of us got turned away, but the white couple didn't. I mean, everybody talks bad about that shelter, because of racism. It's not a secret.

Without talking to the staff members who turned away these clients and without having better data regarding the shelter's intake breakdown along racial, criminal, and addict demographics, it would be presumptuous to conclude that race discrimination definitely took place. However, it should be noted that many homeless people believed racial discrimination was happening and it seemed to them as if the shelter used standards like "criminal" and "addict" as a cover for racial preferences. At the very least, there are real questions that shelter should look to answer. Mainly, (1) who feels welcomed at the shelter and (2) why does the shelter have a negative image regarding racial inclusion?

In addition to perceived discrimination, other barriers to accessing shelters included obtaining photo identification, passing a drug screening through a urine test, and passing a warrant check. While Good Sam's did allow people with criminal records to stay at the shelter, Good Sam's did not permit people to stay who had outstanding warrants or who were convicted of sex offenses. While all of these different types of barriers could sometimes be a hassle, overall, participants stated that they felt a sense of relief once they were admitted to the shelter. Now a part of the shelter, the residents not only enjoyed access to a bed and a roof, but they also felt that they had more access to food, medication, employment services, welfare services, counseling services, toiletries, and clothing. As Brandon explained:

When I got out [of prison] I had no clothes at all except what [the prison] gives you. When you get released from prison, [the prison] gives you a pair of sweat pants, sweat shirt, underwear, and socks, but I didn't have nothing else on the outside so that's all I come out with. But as soon as I got out, the shelter hooked me up. They always had snacks out and stuff like that. When I got there, they automatically gave me extra shoes and socks and underwear and pants. There's always donations that people give out. So all your personal stuff—you know, toothbrushes, underwear— that's always pretty good and that's positive.

While Brandon found all of these services to be helpful, the one thing that remained unclear to him was a basic understanding of the shelter's rules. In short, Brandon felt as if the shelter staff took the rules for granted and simply assumed the clients would comply. For instance, the staff expected clients to clean their rooms, do their chores by 8:00 p.m., obey an 11:00 p.m. curfew, not bring in outside food or drink, not smoke inside, not enter the shelter drunk, not be in the shelter between 1:00 p.m. and 4:00 p.m., and not argue with the staff. However, Brandon said that he had to learn these rules from the other residents. He went on to say that "[the other residents] tell you the rules of the shelter and all that stuff, but I'm still not real sure about what [the staff] wants me to do." Brandon did mention that the staff had "been pretty nice." However, he was anxious about interacting with the staff or asking too many questions because he "had been kicked out" of a different shelter for "some reason" that was still unclear.

Like Brandon, there were other clients who chose to maintain a low profile at the shelter for fear of violating some unknown community norm or fear of giving the wrong impression to shelter staff. When Michael was interviewed, he mentioned that he had not even talked to the caseworkers until the day before our interview because he "didn't even know [he] could talk to them until a few days ago when [he] learned that they could help [him] with housing." Unfortunately, Michael said that he cut the conversation short because "it was moving too fast" and that he "wanted to slow down and hold on because [he] didn't want to mess anything up." Essentially, Michael was getting to the point in his housing application where he would have to disclose his criminal history to the caseworker and he was afraid that once he disclosed this information, the caseworker would no longer want to help him, and would possibly find a way to discharge him from Good Sam's. Ultimately, Michael's situation demonstrated a clear cultural barrier between the caseworkers and the clients. If the caseworker wanted to help Michael make progress, then there needed to be a mutual understanding regarding how personal information might influence the caseworker's ability to help. If the caseworker was willing to help Michael regardless of personal history, then this needed to be stated up front, so that Michael would feel safe disclosing personal information and thus, would be better positioned to receive available benefits.

Beyond negotiating boundaries with staff, participants also had to negotiate boundaries with other residents at the shelter. Most personally, they have to navigate roommate relationships with people whom they may or may not know. In the temporary housing area of Good Sam's (30-day-stay), there were eight rooms that each housed between three and five people. Additionally, the rooms were segregated by gender (unless a couple is married) and, if space was available, families with children were given their own room. Besides these small regulations, most rooms were randomly filled with individual clients based on available space. During the interviews, only one person seemed to accept this inevitable roommate situation at face value. Brandon said:

> Rooming with other people isn't too bad. I'm used to it being in prison. You get bunkmates and all that stuff ... we shared a room and a bunk bed and I'm used to bunk beds and other people being in rooms with me, so it's never been a big problem.

As mentioned, Brandon's attitude was the exception. Every other person spoken to during the interview process talked about the negative aspects of being placed with a roommate that he or she did not know. The most common roommate complaints included bad personal hygiene, unclean living habits, bringing food and drink in the room (fear of attracting bugs or mice), lack of privacy, snoring, and theft.

Even when roommate confrontation could be avoided, there were other concerns about living in a shelter with 20–25 strangers. For example, Ashley flat-out refused to stay at Good Sam's and instead opted to stand at an intersection and collect money every day so that her family could continue to stay at a nearby hotel. Explaining her reasons, Ashley said:

> Having a kid is a huge concern out here. You know, I've heard stories about the Good Samaritan's and some of the people that stay there. You got men sneaking hookers and drugs through the windows at night. A bunch of the people are criminals or addicts. Or at least they were at some point. Plus, the place is just dirty and I don't want my kid around that.

Ashley's concerns, while damning, were not unfounded. Because temporary housing was located in the basement of Good Sam's shelter, the windows to each of the temporary housing rooms were at ground level. In the past, several residents had been caught sneaking people, drugs, and alcohol through those windows. Residents had also been caught sneaking in and out of those windows at night in an effort to avoid curfew violations or to avoid being caught intoxicated by the staff. Because of safety codes, these windows had to remain unobstructed and had to open far enough for a person to get out of the building in the case of an emergency: e.g., a fire. Therefore, it is nearly impossible to curb the types of behavior that caused Ashley's concerns.

As Ashley continued to talk about families and homelessness, Ashley mentioned that she would be open to staying at Good Sam's if her family could stay in transitional housing. Transitional housing is a program that allowed people to stay at Good Sam's for two years and is located upstairs; away from temporary housing. However, Ashley pointed out:

> Good Samaritan's does have transitional housing, but no kids. So even if my husband and I could get in as long-term residents, you can't have kids. So we really need a longer-term place for families, but no one really has one.

Joe, who was living on the streets while his family stayed with his in-laws, shared similar sentiments about adequate shelter for homeless families. Joe said:

> I know of three families that are just out and about right now with no place to go because the shelter don't really work for families. They're better just staying in their car. So, I think they need to make the shelter a lot bigger and just have a place sectioned off for families.

Notably, Ashley, Joe, and Tiffany all mentioned that the Women's Center in Carbondale was a good option for families with children who needed temporary shelter. However, as Ashley mentioned, "they don't take men. So, I'd rather be out here with my family than make us split up."

In all, the shelter system could be a rather complex organism to navigate; especially for those who had never been homeless. There were concerns about safety, transportation, community rules, roommate situations, and family options. While these daily concerns were the main focus for the homeless, there were also larger implications for shelter policies. In short, it is troubling that several of the homeless people observed and interviewed during the summer of 2013 were the same homeless people who had been frequenting and utilizing Good Sam's resources since at least 2009. Quite frankly, it looked as if shelter policies were not helping the homeless transition into independent living. Instead, some of the people had become trapped in the perpetual state of homelessness.

When looking for answers as to why people remain stuck in the system, it is worth revisiting Conover's (1984) notion that the homeless are part of a culture that housed people can never understand. Therefore, some of the help provided by shelters, caseworkers, and government assistance is not necessarily compatible with how some homeless people move through the world. Nor does the help necessarily create a foundation for long-term success. For instance, during her interview, Tiffany lamented the lack of long-term help she was provided to fit her specific goals. As she flung her arms violently into the air, she screamed:

> Yeah, nobody's been asking me what I need! A few places will help you get your birth certificate, social security cards, IDs, driver's license, and they show you some place to live. But they don't help with the financing. Plus there's the first month's rent and security deposit. What am I suppose to do with a place to stay but no way to pay for it? They just tell you that you need a job, but they don't actually help you get a job.

Versions of Tiffany's insight were heard throughout several interviews. There was an agreement among participants that social services often helped with immediate needs such as photo identification and temporary shelter, but without any long-term strategy regarding education, job skills, and employment, many homeless people, including Tiffany, ended up back on the streets within a few short months. As Kristen pointed out:

> If I go to a shelter, I want them to help me get a job. Not just look for a job, but placing me in a job. And they need to extend their stay beyond a few weeks because you can't really get anything done in a few weeks as far as finding a job and getting [housing]. Sure, they'll feed you for a few weeks, but after that, you're out on the street again. So they need to set something up longer than a few weeks so that people can get a job, save some money, and never have to go back [to the shelter].

These ideas speak directly to the conclusions of Lundahl and Wicks (2010) as well as Shipler (2005) who write about the need of equipping the homeless with job training and life-skills (e.g., budgeting, banking, writing a résumé) in an effort to help them live more independently once they leave a shelter system or relinquish government benefits.

Without this type of long-term thinking on the part of social agencies, some of the homeless simply got shuffled from one 30-day shelter to the next without ever obtaining independent living skills.

Navigating Employment

While it may be simple enough to understand how the absence of jobs is a major contributing factor to homelessness (Campbell & Reeves, 1989), understanding the relationship between the homeless and full-time employment can be far more complicated. For instance, one of the obstacles that faced several of the participants was their lack of formal education and/or certification. In the case of Joe, he had an extensive background in auto mechanics that he had acquired from a very young age, and he had "built three cars from the ground up" over the past decade. However, because he had not gone to school and was not a certified mechanic, he could not get hired at any local car repair shops. Joe had tried to enroll in a few "Continuing Your Education classes at John A. [Logan Community College]" during the spring semester of 2013, but he said:

> I don't have the money to go to school right now and I can't get a grant. I tried to get one, but they just said that they can't give me a grant at this time. And that's all I get out them. I probably talked with five or six different people in their mechanic program just so I could start on my certificate, but it's always "We can't give you money at this time." So, pretty much, I've just given up on going back to school right now.

Joe shares his interest in learning a new skill so that he could support his family. However, without money he could not pay for a formal education, and without a formal education, he could not obtain a steady career as a mechanic. Therefore, he was stuck in a situation that had very few options for improvement.

In addition to education and/or certification barriers, there were also barriers with regard to gaps in work history as well as employer internal hiring. Like Joe, Kenneth also had plenty of experience in his chosen profession: the food service industry. As mentioned in Chapter 5, Kenneth had worked delivering pizzas for nine years until he was laid off in 2008. Since he had been laid off, Kenneth continued to put in applications at nearly every restaurant in town with no luck. Describing his experience, Kenneth said:

> Right now, I just try to get out here every day and walk up and down this strip. I usually go and apply for jobs pretty regularly: Burger King, Steak N' Shake, Wendy's, Arby's. Basically all those businesses over there [he points to an area with several restaurants]. I've been up and down this strip a million times applying for jobs. Pretty much, I've been all over town the last four years. I try to put in a new [application] at each location at least every two months, but haven't gotten any calls back yet.

Kenneth's routine was exhausting. He tried to fill out one application every few days and made a schedule so that he could revisit each business once every two months. When asked about why he felt he did not have any success, he said that employers "wanted somebody with recent experience." With the shortage of jobs in southern Illinois, employers could afford to be picky about whom they employed. Even though Kenneth had experience in the food industry, his experience was five years old and if "somebody [already working in food services] wanted that position, then [the employer] had to take them first." Unfortunately, the longer Kenneth remained out of the food service industry, the larger the gap became in his work history, and the harder it would be for him to reenter the work force.

In searching for these types of entry-level jobs that would provide them a steady income over the long-term, participants also negotiated the short-term relationship between the amount of time they had each day to make money, their expected job earnings with a new job, and their current welfare/charity benefits. In short, participants asked themselves, "Is searching for a job worth my time?" or "Will I earn more money if I spend my time panhandling and/or applying for government assistance?" Philip talked at length about this problem and said, "with the time I put out here [panhandling], shit, if I had a job, it'd probably be easier. But I stay out here [panhandling] because I have to make rent at the hotel." Philip went on to say:

> There's no way that I can keep up paying [the hotel rent] daily and try to look for a job at the same time. But [the hotel] don't take no shorts, so [my wife and I] have to make the money every day or our kid'll be out on the streets. [This was before DCFS removed his child from his and his wife's custody, a situation discussed near the end of Chapter 5]. Other than that, if I could get someone to pay up a little bit for me, like a week or two, maybe I could go out and find a job and it wouldn't be a problem. But finding the daily rent is hard, so there ain't no time for jobsearching.

This illustrates the complicated trade-offs of short-term and long-term objectives. Of course Philip would prefer to have a "regular job because just standing out here all day is a shame and embarrassing." However,

116

because panhandling "is a full-time job," it was hard for him to make time to search for employment.

Ultimately, Philip's long-term goal was to find work as a machine operator or a metal worker. Yet, finding this type of work required him to travel dozens of miles out of town just for an interview. Without a car, Philip would have to hitch a ride or buy a bus ticket and probably would have to be away from his wife and child for a few nights while he was traveling. While the transportation and lodging cost would be worth it if he landed a job, his short-term reality required that his family made $46 a day to keep a roof above his little girl's head. Therefore, every day Philip had to choose between panhandling for his (likely) guaranteed income and searching for a job. If he did not panhandle and could not secure an immediate job, he faced eviction for not coming up with the day's rent. For those who spend so much time searching for immediate resources in order to survive, it is difficult to figure out where they might find the time to obtain job skills, further their education, and/or apply for employment; especially if any of these endeavors require a great amount of transportation or financial investment.

In all, Joe was the only participant spoken to who was willing to make the financial investment to travel a great distance on the hope that he *might* find employment working for a semi-truck company in Indiana. Discussing his upcoming travels, Joe said:

> At this point I've got nothing else to lose. I'm leaving Saturday and that's why I'm out here now [panhandling]. I need to make $300 between now and Saturday to go to Indiana. It's $137 for [the orientation class] and then food for three weeks because I don't get paid for three weeks if I get on a crew.

At the time of this interview, there was no guarantee that Joe would be hired by the semi-truck company nor did Joe have a clear understanding about what he would be doing for the company. He had made contact with the company through his cousin, and based on his phone conversation with the employer, the company had training programs for drivers, loaders, and warehouse workers. In truth, Joe did not want to travel so far away from his family for a job opportunity that might not work out, but as he told it:

> I don't have much of a choice but to go and do it. Don't neither [my wife or I] want it to happen, but we can't keep going like this either. Even if I get on, I don't want to do it because I'll be gone all the time [from my family]. I mean, it'll pretty much be like it is now with me not really seeing my kids. Either I'll be living and working in

Indiana at the warehouse or the best thing would be that I get to be a driver. But even then [drivers are] gone eight days and then home for two ... and on some jobs I could stay out for as much as three months at a time. But I don't want to do that 'cause I have three kids. But what other choice do I have?

Quite frankly, Joe did not have much of choice if he wanted a chance at securing employment and reestablishing some financial stability for his family. He had exhausted all of his leads in southern Illinois and now had to look for employment elsewhere, even if that meant crossing state lines. Yet, even these efforts did not guarantee him work, and after spending $300 on travel and expenses, he might end up back where he started.

In all of the aforementioned cases, there were unique situational barriers that made it difficult for Joe, Kenneth, and Philip to become gainfully employed: lack of education, lack of current work experience, lack of transportation, and the need to negotiate short-term needs with long-term goals. Additionally, some participants, such as Maddy, said they needed more access to "computers and the internet because all the jobs are online." She went on to say that she would like to use computers to find job openings, fill out applications, take employment tests for different companies, and research different companies so that she felt more confident going into interviews.

Others, like James, were concerned about overcoming strongly-held prejudices from potential employers. As James put it, "It's not like companies are just out here handing out jobs to homeless people." Instead, "They'd rather take a chance with a college kid who has a legitimate address." Truthfully, it should be recognized that some of the employment barriers some homeless people faced stemmed from previous actions of their own, such as dropping out of high school, past drug addiction, or having a criminal record. Understandably, it might also be challenging for some people to feel empathy for those who cannot get a job because of these types of behaviors. Yet, this research suggests that it is unwise for society to let sophomoric mistakes permanently prevent a person from entering the workforce. Instead, it might be more productive to help the homeless find meaningful ways of supporting themselves on a path toward financial stability and housing independence. Otherwise, it is likely that some of them will end up permanently homeless, uneducated, without job skills, and completely reliant on social services.

One possible solution to the unique employment challenges faced by the homeless was offered by Philip. Because Philip felt like he always had to negotiate the finite amount of time he had to search for a job, panhandle, and apply for government assistance, Philip said that it might be better if the government simply provided homeless people "a house to stay in while [they] worked [for the government]" instead of providing homeless people with monetary benefits. At the time of our interview, Philip did receive food stamps, but did not receive cash benefits, for which he was qualified, because the cash benefits welfare program required him "to volunteer 35 hours a week for only $300 a month" in assistance. Philip went on to say that he "made more money just panhandling" and therefore, there was no incentive for him to apply for cash benefits. In laying out his plan, Philip said:

> It would be nice if the government had some assistance program where at least you could work for them for your rent; for your place to stay. Like I can go out and do work cleaning parks, or streets, or washing windows and they can put me in housing or in the projects instead of paying me. You know, I'd swap work for rent. That'd be a good idea for [the government], too. They don't have to give me no cash and, I mean, there's plenty of housing units. Hey, that's a good idea! Yeah, I should write somebody about that. That's a pretty good idea [laughs]!

Philip also mentioned that it would be a good idea for the homeless shelters to adopt a similar policy "instead of having an open door policy" because people need to "be motivated to help themselves out" and should "contribute to the shelter by working."

Whether Philip's plan would work is yet to be determined. However, Philip's insight and creativity might help bring policymakers closer to solving three major concerns with regard to the homeless and employment. First, homeless people who signed up for Philip's program would no longer have to worry about securing shelter on a daily basis. Hopefully, this would relieve some housing anxiety and allow people to concentrate on other issues such as furthering education and developing new job skills. Second, Philip's program could help people develop new job skills, which would put them in a better position for achieving full-time employment. Granted, much of the work Philip described would be entry-level custodial work. However, even these types of entry-level jobs are constantly changing with new technologies, machines, and operating procedures. Plus, these types of entry-level jobs put people in the position to eventually become crew supervisors and managers. Finally, Philip's program would help homeless people avoid long droughts in their employment history. Avoiding long droughts in one's work history would hopefully show a potential employer that the person is motivated and willing to work. Of course, there are potential downsides to Philip's idea, such as loss of work for current city employees who perform custodial work and there is even the risk of the government exploiting the homeless for cheap labor. However, given Philip's in-depth knowledge about his experiences with being homeless and looking for work, it is important to seriously engage these types of creative ideas that are *generated by the homeless* in an effort to find long-term solutions to the unemployment problem that plagues the homeless community. Ultimately, policies generated within the homeless community provide knowledge to policymakers about what the homeless community needs to be successful as well as gives the homeless a sense of ownership over the policies that dictate their daily lives.

Navigating Charity

Absent of any current long-term employment strategies, all of the homeless people interviewed spent a substantial part of their days navigating charitable donations to help supplement their daily needs such as food, clothing, and shelter. These charitable donations came from large organizations such as churches and shelters as well as individuals such as family, friends, and strangers on the streets. In seeking out charitable donations, participants had to overcome three distinct obstacles. The first obstacle was personal pride. All told, it should be noted that not a single homeless person talked to enjoyed asking people for help. Kristen succinctly summed up this sentiment when she said, "I don't want to ask anybody for help. I hate it. I hate asking people for help." In addition to Kristen's comments, several others described asking for help as "embarrassing," "shameful," and "degrading." In particular, the men viewed receiving charity as an indictment of their masculinity by calling attention to their failures as fathers, sons, and overall providers. As Brandon mentioned, "I'm a 38-year-old man now and should be able to take care of myself."

Despite feelings of inadequacy, all participants eventually swallowed their pride and sought help from charitable organizations. In turn, finally seeking out help presented new obstacles. Mainly, the second obstacle participants talked about was being denied services because of certain organizational policies. This seemed to be most prevalent among faith-based charities such as churches. As Kenneth put it:

> Most [churches] don't want to help you unless you are a member. Like some have a food pantry and you can get food there, but that's basically it. But when I tried to get my apartment, I tried to get a deposit from them, but I couldn't. Members can get help with bills and stuff, but I couldn't because I'm not a member.

To be fair, Kenneth was introspective and theorized that perhaps many churches had limited funds and therefore "helping their members first" seemed reasonable.

Beyond churches, some secular organizations also had policies that kept certain participants from receiving support. For example, Joe was unable to obtain a security deposit for a family-unit apartment because his wife and children were staying with her parents and therefore, his "family was not technically homeless" according to the organization. Additionally, a non-profit organization denied Brandon a $25 security deposit for public housing because he had a felony record. According to Brandon:

> No one's really helped me with filling out an application or getting a deposit. They might tell you a few things about *how* to get one, but no one will help you with [the deposit]. If I didn't have the felony that I do, I think more people might be able to help me with the rent. But there's other people without felonies, so I get pushed to the back of the line.

All told, charitable organizations have the right to create policies that they believe are beneficial to their mission, their staff, and their clientele. Whether these policies are reasonable is truly a matter of personal opinion. However, what cannot be ignored is the fact that certain policies regarding declarations of faith, family status, and criminal record are denying some homeless people access to certain services. At the very least, organizations should recognize the structural barriers faced by some homeless people because of certain policies and perhaps look into creating new policies that will provide more opportunities for more homeless people to access services.

The third, and final, obstacle participants faced when trying to obtain charitable services was government ordinances. Similar to the ordinances described in the literature review (see Feldman, 2004;

Flaccus, 2012; "Homeless Camping," 2012), participants in this study had been cited for vagrancy, panhandling, consuming alcohol in public, and sleeping in public. In one uniquely ironic situation, Kenneth was cited four times in one day by the police after he called the police for help. Explaining the incident Kenneth said:

> I did come across a guy out here about a week ago. He come up and he was hollering at me through the McDonald's parking lot. I couldn't hear him and he got closer and said, "I'm asking you a question!" I'm like, "What?" He said, "Did you hurt that kid's arm?" I said, "No." And he started yelling that I was always out here trying to get money and no one else could panhandle in this spot and finally he picked up a damn rock and threw it at me and then started saying that he was going to stab me. So I ended up running to get a phone and calling the cops. And that got me in trouble because I was out here panhandling and the cops were trying to shut [panhandlers] down.

In the end, Kenneth said that the police never tried to get information about the man who was responsible for threatening Kenneth and that the police seemed more interested in getting the homeless to stop panhandling than catching violent agitators. The police returned to Kenneth's corner three more times that day and Kenneth "ended up with four tickets" for panhandling. According to Kenneth, two of the tickets had already been dropped, but the other two carried $125 fines. Because Kenneth was unable to pay the tickets, he had "to go to court soon" where he faced possible jail time.

When Ashley faced a similar situation with the police, she decided to push back. Well aware of her legal rights to panhandle, Ashley told the police:

> "If you're standing on a corner holding a sign—not verbalizing any request—then that's okay." But the cops didn't like my attitude and I got four tickets altogether. You see, approaching people is illegal, but we were just standing there with our signs. And we were just trying to stay out of trouble and the police said, "Well, I can make trouble for you." You know, it was just really harassing. Then [the police] got real aggravated because we knew our rights and they were like "Well, it's going to cost you $150 to pay your fine and I'll just keep writing tickets until you go to jail."

Fortunately, Ashley found an advocate in a local city council member. She contacted Councilman Don Monty to see whether her panhandling was illegal and, according to Ashley, Monty told her that "what you are doing is fine." After a few phone calls, the tickets were finally dropped and Ashley is "sure that the cops are kind of pissed off because Don Monty did take those tickets away" [laughs]! Ashley concluded her story by saying, "You have to make sure to write a 'thank you' from us to Mr. Monty. He's as cool as a cucumber and he really went to bat for us. If it wasn't for him, we wouldn't be out here."

While not all advocates are as well connected as Councilman Don Monty, the homeless do come in contact with charitable citizens nearly every day. As Ashley stated, "People can be really generous. I've got people who go to the store and hook me up with food when we got nothing to eat. And they give me clothes in the winter for my daughter." Furthermore, Kenneth admitted:

> Life isn't all bad. I've got a few people who stop by regularly. If they see me around town, they'll stop by. I got one lady I know that stopped by the other night and she gave me a milkshake 'cause it was pretty hot out. I probably see her once a week.

Joe also shared a story about a person who regularly stopped by to check on him. Joe said:

> He asked if I was staying in a hotel and I told him "No." "Well," he said, "put your sign down and I'll take you back and pay for your room." So he took me back and we got to talkin' about my kids and the story must have touched him because he ended up givin' me $300 to pay for the whole week! He said, "Well, at least you're being a man, you know, don't feel too bad about what you're doing out here because you're trying to do right by your kids. A lot of guys would fly the coop, but I'm gonna give you this and pray for you because you're sticking up and being a father."

These types of experiences illustrated the impact that personal relationships between homeless people and non-homeless people had with regard to helping participants access food, clothing, and shelter. Additionally, while the material goods were necessary in order to survive the day-to-day struggles, Joe also mentioned that "sometimes it's just nice to talk to someone who will listen."

Finally, it should be noted that participants were quick to pile on endless amounts of appreciation for all forms of charity. This appreciation was in response to large offerings such as hotel bills as well as small offerings such as spare change and half-eaten sandwiches. Markedly, participants discussed two important reasons for offering appreciation. First, participants recognized the potential sacrifices that went into the charitable giving. These sacrifices might have included volunteer hours, clothing donations, food donations, and monetary donations. Additionally, participants recognized that these sacrifices might have caused temporary hardship for the person offering help. For instance, Philip stated:

> Even if they only give you a couple of pennies or part of a sandwich you say "thank you" because maybe that's all they got. Maybe they just gave you their lunch for the

day and now they can't eat. So you don't want to tear people down because you don't know what they're going through. I've been torn down. I don't want to do that to other people. So always be polite and appreciate what other people give you.

Second, participants offered appreciation because even the smallest donation helped alleviate some level of anxiety and hardship. In speaking about how much she appreciated the smallest donations, Maddy energetically stated:

I appreciate pennies. I don't care. A can of soup. People can give me food they have cleaned out the refrigerator. Hell, I'd appreciate that. I just want everyone to know how much I appreciate everything. Even if it is just a few pennies or a half-a-sandwich. I was standing out here the other day and somebody said, "All I have is some water that I already drank out of." Man, I will take it. I'm so thirsty out here. I'm a beggar and I can't be a chooser.

In the end, participants were well aware of their dire circumstances and understood that they were often at the mercy of other people's ability and willingness to give. This not only placed the participants in a position of intense vulnerability, but also placed them in a position to be extremely grateful for even the smallest offerings. Therefore, seemingly insignificant charitable donations such as half-eaten food, spare change, and used clothing really did make the difference in someone's day.

Navigating Government Assistance

The final area participants found themselves navigating was the tangled web of government assistance. In total, participants emphasized four main programs within government assistance that held the most influence in their lives: housing, unemployment insurance, disability insurance, and food stamps. Five participants briefly mentioned medical coverage such as Medicaid, but nothing substantive was said about the process of receiving this form of government assistance.

To be fair, many participants, like Ashley, said:

The process to get public aid has gotten easier. I have a thirteen-year-old daughter and when I first applied when she was a baby, I had to go into the office to apply for the medical and food stamps. And I had to be interviewed in the office and fill out paperwork there. But now you can do it over the phone or mail it in. So, since I don't have transportation, it's much easier.

However, Ashley went on to say that "financially, there's just no resources." This sentiment was shared by all participants. While everyone interviewed was actively seeking out more government assistance, each participant lamented the fact that benefits were being cut and that the screening process for some programs could take months or even years. In other cases, applicants were flat-out denied before they could even fill out the paperwork. This was the situation Tiffany faced when she attempted to enroll in public housing.

At first, Tiffany did not want to enroll in public housing. She had worked all her life, but after an injury she lost her job at a factory and the medical bills began piling up. Some of her expenses were turned over to a collection agency and her "credit [score] tanked overnight." With regard to housing, Tiffany said, "trying to get help finding a place to stay has been the biggest challenge because if you don't have good credit you're basically screwed anymore because [landlords] do credit checks." Tiffany eventually decided to try public housing, but immediately found out that she did not qualify because she was a convicted felon. During the interview, she asked:

> What are [felons] supposed to do? They won't hire you. It's hard to find a place to live. I don't know what they expect us to do. And some of [the crimes] are honest mistakes. I can understand that if you're a felon and it's a gun charge or you're a pedophile, but little misdemeanors and felonies like drug possession charges?

Tiffany said that she was charged and convicted for possession of "just one hit worth of heroin" over 15 years ago. She spent "only a few nights in jail" and was put on probation for two years. Tiffany said that this was the only time she had ever been convicted of a crime and that she has been clean ever since.

Once again, Tiffany's story brings to light essential questions regarding homeless people who committed crimes, served time, and have not committed any crimes since being released. Without some type of process that can help reintegrate homeless people who are convicted felons into jobs and housing, many convicted felons without financial resources, education, or job skills will remain homeless with dismal opportunities for regaining independent living.

That being said, even participants who did not have felony convictions sometimes found it difficult to navigate the public housing application process. For example, both Ashley and Kristen had applied multiple times for public housing, but had so far been unsuccessful in receiving aid. Ashley claimed that "the waiting list is five miles long" and that she had "never been able to sign up for [public housing] because [the waiting list had] always been closed every time [she] tried to sign up." Kristen did say that she had made it onto the waiting list in May 2013, but that the government worker who helped her fill out the application told her that "it would be 18 months before something opened up." What made Kristen's public housing application process even more complicated was that she was currently looking for a job. She had gone through the résumé process and was waiting to hear back from the employer, but Kristen was hesitant about the job opportunity because "once [she] start[ed] this job, [she was] going to lose [her] spot in line" on the public housing waiting list.

In short, public housing has certain income thresholds that applicants must fall below. Given that some waiting lists are 18-months long, it is easy to see why some applicants would be hesitant about taking an entry-level job while they are on the waiting list. For instance, Kristen might take the job and earn enough money to make her ineligible for public housing. Consequently, she would be removed from the waiting list. If she happened to lose the job shortly thereafter (she might not be able to perform the job and, in turn, get fired), then she would have to reapply for housing and her application would be placed at the end of the line where she would have to start the 18 month waiting period all over. Ultimately, one of the problems seems to be that public housing applications do not account for fluctuating incomes and/or job searches over the course of 18 months. If the goal is to help people obtain financial independence, then people like Kristen should not feel conflicted about "keeping her spot in line" or looking for work. Instead, Kristen should have felt empowered to start working without fearing that her application would be sent to the back of the line because she suddenly made too much money. This does not mean that Kristen should get to save her spot in line indefinitely nor does it mean that Kristen should have received public housing if she could support herself. However, perhaps the application screening process might think about saving spots on the waiting list for six to twelve months for people who are adjusting to jobs they have found during the application process. Conceivably, the security of knowing that their spots would be saved while they attempted to obtain long-term employment might be enough to encourage people like Kristen to take advantage of more employment opportunities.

Unlike Kristen, most of the participants in this study had no prospects for employment opportunities. This situation encouraged participants to file for unemployment insurance or disability insurance. Unemployment insurance is a government benefit provided to people who are currently unemployed and looking for work ("Unemployment Insurance," 2014). In contrast, disability insurance is a government benefit provided to people who are currently unemployed and cannot work ("Disability Insurance," 2014). While these two government assistance programs are supposed to address the needs of two different demographics, during this research it was discovered that among some beneficiaries, these two programs are often used in tandem with one another.

A 2012 report from the Government Accountability Office found that "in fiscal year 2010, 117,000 individuals received concurrent cash benefit payments from the Disability Insurance (DI) and Unemployment Insurance (UI) programs of more than $850 million..." ("Income Security," 2012, para. 1).

The most common way participants became involved with both programs was by starting off with unemployment insurance and then trying to move onto disability insurance once unemployment insurance benefits ran out. Kenneth explained the reasoning for this when he stated:

> Unemployment is probably the most beneficial in terms of getting money quick and easy. All you really need to do is show them that you had a job and now you don't. I lived off unemployment for the first couple of years after I lost my job and then that run out. I tried using computers [at the library] to look for a job. I've been to Manpower, but they've basically shut down unless you have an appointment. So, then I just applied for disability. Disability is a lot harder to prove and it took a few months before I got a check, but now at least I have a little bit of income.

Even though disability insurance is meant to provide benefits to people who cannot work, Kenneth was looking for a job during the time of the interview and said that he "would take any job [he] could get." Similar to Kenneth, Brandon was also trying to utilize both insurance programs even though the programs were designed to fit the needs of two different demographics. Unlike Kenneth, Brandon was denied unemployment the first time he applied because he had recently been released from prison and therefore, had no immediate prior work history. While his unemployment insurance claim was in appeal, Brandon decided to apply for disability although he admitted that he wasn't *"really* disabled" [emphasis in the original]. However, because he needed income, he thought it was a good idea to "apply for everything and see what [he got]." Brandon also mentioned that "disability takes forever; something like six months to a year," but went on to say that the wait was worth it because he "had to get something; disabled or not."

In contrast to Kenneth and Brandon, Tiffany could not work because she injured her back in 2008. She ended up having a $400,000 back surgery in 2009, but the surgery could only correct so much and Tiffany was left with "permanent nerve damage in [her] left leg" and could "no longer feel [her] left foot." Tiffany lost her job and had been in and out of homelessness ever since. If Tiffany was able to collect disability, she would be able to move into an apartment. However, she had been waiting for her disability insurance application to be accepted for five years and was no longer confident that it would ever be processed. When asked why it was taking so long, she said:

> The hold-up is because everybody that applies to disability is denied the first time. Then you have to appeal it. So, it's a long process waiting for the appeals to go through and a decision to be made whether you're disabled or not. For me, I can't work anymore and I'm eventually going to lose my left leg. Some people wait months for disability. Some people wait years. It just depends on how quickly they can verify your condition.

Listening to Tiffany talk about the appeals process, it is impossible not to think about how her situation was directly affected by Kenneth's and Brandon's actions. In short, disability insurance personnel had to take their time verifying Tiffany's claim because other applicants had attempted to collect benefits for which they were not entitled. This added scrutiny slowed the process and created life-changing circumstances for Tiffany, such as loss of income, poverty, and homelessness.

While it would be easy, and justified, to blame people like Kenneth and Brandon who abused certain benefits and made it harder for others to collect, there are also bigger structural concerns that should not be ignored. For example, while Kenneth was receiving unemployment, why weren't there job-training requirements in place to ensure that he had a job opportunity once his unemployment benefits ran out? Furthermore, why didn't the unemployment application process and the disability application process make it clear to Brandon that he could not benefit from these programs concurrently? While Brandon's disability application may ultimately be denied, the fact that his application is in the system and needs to be processed means that the disability insurance process will be slowed down for others. If his application is accepted, then there will be less money in the program for other beneficiaries. Notably, in June 2013, there was bipartisan legislation introduced in the United States Senate entitled the "Reducing Overlapping Payment Act" that at least began a conversation about how to end the practice of people trying to benefit from unemployment and disability in tandem. As Senator Jeff Flake from Arizona put it, these types of reforms are needed to bring "greater solvency to the disability insurance program which so many Americans truly in need depend on" ("Senators Introduce," 2013, para. 3). In the long term, perhaps creating a process that only allows people to apply for one benefit program at a time and forbids people from jumping from one program to the next would decrease the number of applications each program processes and allow people like Tiffany to have their applications processed much more quickly.

The final government assistance program participants discussed was food stamps. Distinctly, all 10 participants reported receiving food stamps, making food stamps the most widely-utilized form of government assistance within this study. Additionally, the reported benefits participants received from food stamps ranged from $100–$300 per month and depended on a participant's monthly income and family size. For example, the four single men in the study each reported receiving about $200 a month in food assistance. Arguably, this seemed like an adequate amount of money for a single man's monthly food bill. However, the process of using food stamps as a homeless person usually meant that he only ate once or twice a day (unless he was staying at a shelter) and he often went without food during the last few days of the month.

This reality makes more sense as Michael explains his daily food routine:

> Eating out here ends up being like eight or ten dollars a day. And [food stamps] are kind of worthless because you can't take food anywhere to store it and cook it. So you have to buy something that's already made. Like I'll go and get a six dollar salad at Schnuck's and like three or four dollars worth of meat from the deli and eat it right then and there. It should stretch out a lot more. Like eight or ten dollars should last three days at home, but you have to eat all at once out here because you can't take food anywhere. You can't take it to a refrigerator. You can't save it. I don't have a kitchen and they don't let you bring food into Good Sam's. So you can only buy what you can eat at the store, which is the expensive premade stuff.

Michael went on to say that when he first received his food stamp card he ate three meals a day from the Schnuck's grocery store. However:

> I ran out of money in like two weeks. So, you learn to eat once a day because you can't financially afford to eat three times a day or you'll drain your card [that provides people in Illinois with food stamp benefits]. Just imagine having eight dollar charges three times a day. You'll be broke really quickly.

Michael's process of buying food-as-needed was not only common among the participants, but was also the most expensive way of purchasing food. Instead of purchasing in bulk, participants bought premade meals and often threw out the leftovers.

Besides cost, there were also discussions about nutrition. For example, several participants did not have transportation to a grocery store and therefore, used their food stamps at nearby gas stations to purchase snack foods such as soda, chips, candy, and microwavable burritos. Brandon said that he likes to walk down to the Circle K because he "can get hot food there" with his chips and grape soda. As a government regulation, food stamps cannot be used to purchase hot food. However, Brandon, and others, had found a loophole. Essentially, he *first* purchases a frozen burger, burrito, taco, etc., from the gas station and *then* heats it up in the gas station's microwave. While the nutritional options at a gas station are far scarcer compared to a grocery store, Brandon's meal still cost him "about six dollars." In the end, just eating this one modest meal every day for a month could cost Brandon $180 of a $200 food stamp limit. These types of margins leave virtually no room for fulfilling meals or adequate nutrition for a homeless person who has no way to store food and no way to cook food. In the end, this food assistance structure seemed beneficial to no one. Not only were homeless people still hungry and eating packaged food, but government assistance was being used on food in the most expensive way imaginable: one microwavable burrito at a time.

7. Manipulating the System

Deanna came running into the shelter out of breath with a coy smile across her face. "Holy hell!" she shouted as she bent over to rest her hands on her knees and catch her breath. Deanna was always participating in harmless mischief so I had to ask her, "What did you do this time?" "I came about this close to going to jail," she said while making a visual gesture with her thumb and index finger. She went on to explain that she had been down at the Circle K convenience store trying to sell off the remaining balance of her food stamps when an off-duty police officer interrupted her deal. Her plan was to sell the remaining balance of $50 for $25 and put the money toward a bus ticket. The cop told her that bargaining government benefits was illegal (which she knew), but that "he wasn't going to bother writing [her] up because [selling food stamps] happens all the time."

While getting caught selling $50 worth of food stamps would probably not lead to jail time in most circumstances, Deanna was currently on parole. So, if she got caught doing anything illegal, she would most likely go back to jail. Furthermore, while highlighting Deanna's ploy to obtain $25 cash from selling food stamps may seem trivial and insignificant, her story actually illustrates a very significant example as to how some homeless people survive on a daily basis. Twenty-five dollars may not seem like a lot of money when one considers the billions of dollars spent on government assistance programs, but to a person who has no financial stability, $25 can go a long way. Arguably, these types of nickel-and-dime hustles shape a large portion of some homeless people's financial livelihood. Therefore, in an effort to better understand homelessness, it is important to discuss both the honest and dishonest ways homeless people acquire and utilize resources.

Understandably, talking about government benefit abuse among the poor can be controversial and unpopular. However, abuse does happen (see Briquelet, 2013; see Hall, 2012; see "Profits from Poverty," 2012). Therefore, in the interest of conveying a more complete narrative about the lived experiences of homeless people, it is important that this research presents both the stories that give us hope as well as the stories that make us uncomfortable. As mentioned previously, when telling stories about benefit abuse it is not the intention to blame the homeless for abusing the system. Instead, these stories are brought to light because they give us a more complete picture of homelessness and thus, can guide us toward creating better policies that more adequately address the needs of the homeless community. Accordingly, this chapter draws attention to how the participants of this study manipulated, abused, cheated, lied, and committed fraud in order to acquire different types of benefits. Words like "abused" and "cheated" aren't meant to judge people's actions, but only to describe the behavior. Furthermore, this is the type of language used by some participants when talking about the choices they make. For example, when talking about selling government cell phones, James said, "It's cheatin' the government, but they owe me!"

In working through the various forms of deceit, Chapter 7 is organized into three different sections. First, it discusses how some homeless people abuse government benefits. Second, it talks about the different ways some homeless people scam charity. Finally, it points out the different types of deception that happen within homeless shelters.

Manipulating the Government

As a person who had known Deanna for a number of years, Michael had seen Deanna sell her food stamp benefits at local gas stations several times. Michael was interviewed the day after Deanna had tried to sell her food stamps at the Circle K and he referred to Deanna as "just another professional hobo." While critical of her actions, Michael was also protective of Deanna, as if she were his younger sibling. For instance, Michael said:

> It's easy for me to say this stuff about her because I've known her for so long. But no one else better talk bad about her [smiles]. You see, she's always running the system

looking for the next handout. Like, I think that if you have a Link card for more than a year, there's something wrong with you. But she's pretty much been on that card her whole life. Now, come on, you don't need no Link card for 25 years. She's not crippled or nothing. If you do, then fuck you. You ain't trying to be productive. I understand some people can't work and, I'll be generous, maybe you need [a Link card] for *five years* if you have kids. But [Deanna] doesn't have any kids. That lady you saw running in here yesterday—she's just another professional hobo [laughs].

In discussing Deanna's actions, Michael's words hint at the complicated relationship between individual and systemic accountability (see Evans, 1988). At the individual level, the obvious critique is to fault Deanna for excessively using a taxpayer-funded program and for illegally selling her benefits. However, at the systemic level, critics might ask why a government program allowed a 25-year-old, able-bodied woman to continuously receive food stamps without any educational intervention or workforce training, which could have led to financial independence. As noted by Evans (1988), personal and collective actions create a system that allows for the existence of homelessness. Deanna might have acted dishonestly, but the system allowed her to act dishonestly without consequence. Therefore, there were no incentives for her to change her actions. Without accountability, personal and collective actions don't change, and the vicious cycle of homelessness continues.

Like Deanna, other homeless people also admitted to selling food stamps for cash. For instance, Brandon and Maddy used the same Circle K convenience store to sell their food stamps so they could buy personal items such as soap, shampoo, razors, tissue, toilet paper, and cigarettes. At the time of the interviews, each was adamant that the cash received from selling food stamps was not being used to purchase alcohol or drugs. Although Maddy did admit that when she was 20 "there were plenty of times when [she] would bust off a couple ounces of cocaine" after cashing in her food stamps. When asked about why they decided to sell their food stamps, Brandon and Maddy both agreed that food stamps were essentially worthless since they were able to eat three meals a day at Good Sam's. However, according to Maddy, when a person is homeless "it's hard to come by good razors and good-smelling shampoo." Effectively, Brandon's and Maddy's needs were not being met through government assistance and they found that bargaining with food stamps, while illegal, was a reasonable way to acquire desired resources. Converting food stamps into cash simply made sense given the current situation.

When Brandon was pressed about the illegal behavior, the interview shifted towards questions that asked about "how complicated," "how secretive," and "how careful" people were when selling benefits. Brandon looked rather confused about this type of phrasing and said, "No man. There's just a guy around the corner. It's no big secret. Everybody knows him. I can put you in contact with him if you need some cash." Brandon's whole attitude about the process was surprisingly nonchalant and commonplace. He finished his explanation by saying that the guy around the corner "deals with someone higher up so everybody gets a cut. I give him $100 worth of food stamps and he gives me sixty bucks. It's kinda like drugs, but it's in the open and no one gets shot [laughs]." While a few other people who sold their Link cards on the streets were approached for informal interviews, this research was never able to track down the cards' final destinations. The only two conclusions that can be made are that the dealers used them to purchase food, which is unlikely given the assumed quantity of cards bought, or the dealers resold the cards for a profit.

As this research soon found out, dealing Link cards was just one of the ways people bent the rules in an effort to acquire cash through selling government benefits. Like the Link card dealers who bought and sold food stamps, there were also cell phone dealers like James. James first became aware that the government supplied free cell phones to poor people in 2012 when he reapplied for food stamps. Before 2012, James remembered having to apply for each benefit separately. Now, if James applied for one service, such as food stamps, the social service worker automatically started to ask him about other services for which he may be eligible. As James mentioned, "I got one of those government phones. I be texting on it all the time. I mean, it's free." While the intention of the free phones is to provide poor people with a lifeline in case of emergencies and perhaps to contact loved ones or set up job interviews, James discovered that selling government cell phones was a profitable side business. James said:

> I really found out by accident. I was back here and Nate kept asking me to use my phone, but I didn't want to let him because I really didn't know him. But then I did and he took off and I never saw him again. Anyway, I called the cell phone office to say it was stolen and they just gave me another one.

The ease with which James was able to obtain another government-funded cell phone gave him the idea to sell his cell phone every couple of months and then report it stolen. For his efforts, he only makes about $20 per phone, but since he "didn't pay for them anyway, it's all profit." As for his customers, James said they are only able to use the phone for about a month until service is turned off. When asked why his customers paid him $20 instead of just getting their own free cell phone, James discussed three possible reasons. First, some people do not know the phones are free. Second, some people do not qualify for free phones and buying a $20 "burner phone" is easier and cheaper than getting an actual cell phone plan. Three, some people have criminal records or warrants and want to stay under the radar.

In all, the biggest motivator that drove this type of dishonest behavior seemed to be the participants' perception that qualifying for and collecting benefits was easy. As previously quoted in Chapter 6, Ashley mentioned that "the process to get public aid has gotten easier." However, Tiffany talked about what she saw as a downside to this more convenient system. Tiffany said:

> Yeah, you got people like [José Thomas and Prince Riley]. They've been getting checks every month for disability. They don't need to be homeless, but they're wasting all their money on alcohol and drugs. Everybody knows [José] is an alcoholic, but they just keep giving him money because disability is automatic. It's not like they evaluate him every year. He just keeps getting it until he tells [the government] to stop. And ain't no one's gonna tell [the government] to stop sending them a free check. And it makes the public think that all homeless people are bums or alcoholics or addicts and we're not.

José and Prince were not residents at the shelter, but they did come in for meals a couple of times per week. According to Prince, he received about $1,000 per month through disability, but had been homeless for about "four or five years." Unfortunately, without accountability José and Prince will most likely continue to use their government benefits to support habits that will drain their finances and keep them homeless.

Michael shared similar frustrations about an enabling system when discussing the pressure he felt from a caseworker to sign up for disability even though he did not feel he was disabled. Michael said:

> Not everyone who is homeless is qualified for disability. I think they're qualified to get a fucking job, but you got people like this lazy caseworker pushing everyone to disability because it's easier than helping me get a job. Shit, I'm the last person who wants a handout. But people keep using [disability] as a crutch. Everyone is just hanging out waiting for help with their disability form.... If people aren't working, it's

really their own fault, but then again, who's going to hire someone who's been playing the system for ten or fifteen years. Shit, some of them make more money sitting on their ass collecting disability than working for $9 an hour.

Again, in reporting these observations, it is not my intention to demonize those homeless people who misuse government resources. In fact, in Michael's case, he places some of the blame on a caseworker when talking about filing disability applications under false pretenses. Quite rightly, he asked, "Why does she think she's *knows* I'm disabled? She's not a doctor."

Therefore, instead of demonizing the homeless for exploiting loopholes in the system, this research continues to lean on Evans's (1988) idea that homelessness exists because personal behaviors *and collective institutions* create an environment that leads to poor choices and unintended outcomes. Ironically, free cell phone peddler James fully understood how personal choices and bad policy trapped people in homelessness. James said, "I've been around [homeless] people for 30 years. They're always doing the same shit and they'll keep doing the same shit as long as you allow it." For these reasons, it is imperative to create policies that will encourage the homeless to learn skills that can lead to long-term financial independence (Olasky, 1992) instead of supporting policies that incite them to barter food stamps, peddle government cell phones, and exaggerate disability forms for short-term financial gains.

Manipulating Charity

In addition to government benefit abuse, some homeless people abused charity through exaggeration and dishonesty. According to the participants, they did not act dishonestly to be malicious, but rather dishonesty was "sometimes necessary" in order to survive the daily grind of being homeless. Rather bluntly, Ashley remarked that "you can't just make it on the government. You can't. So, you have to find other ways to scrape together money." The most common way participants abused charity was by taking advantage of sympathetic friends and family members.

Consider Kenneth's story. Because Kenneth had experience in the service industry, he knew several people in Carbondale who worked as custodians, maintenance workers, and house-keepers at local hotels. He was able to use these connections to get a good deal at a hotel, but after a few nights he ran out of money. Kenneth continued:

> I got in pretty good with the assistant manager at this hotel, and since John [the custodian] knew me, the manager let me slide on the rent for a couple of nights. He kinda started a tab for me. But then it got to where I was owing so much money that he said "You gotta go." Well, I didn't want to go because it was cold. So I made him feel bad about throwing me out and he gave me a couple more days to get the money together, but I eventually just ducked out early and never paid him.

Kenneth went on to say that "this type of thing happened" at several other hotels and that it ultimately ended his friendship with John. According to Kenneth, John said that Kenneth "took advantage" of their friendship and "made him look like an asshole in front of his boss." Furthermore, John said that Kenneth would have "figured out how to get the money" if he really cared about John. These types of "taking advantage" narratives were common among participants who had experienced strained relationships with friends and family members. Unsurprisingly, the pattern of each narrative was similar. First, a person would become homeless. Second, the homeless person's family and friends would help out him or her. Third, according to the family or friends, the homeless person would "take advantage" of the resources by staying at a friend's house for too long, using money for drugs or alcohol, not looking for a job, disappearing for several days, or lying about where money was going. Finally, the relationship would dissolve.

In the case of Ashley, her relationship with her father dissolved after she improperly used the charity her father afforded her through his retirement account. According to Ashley, she was supposed to use the money her father gave her to take some additional college courses so she could get a new job that was not physically demanding (with respect to Ashley's back injury). But Ashley "stopped going to school halfway through the term" and used the rest of her tuition money to buy food, Christmas presents for her daughter, and winter clothing for her family. Upset that Ashley used the money on "unnecessary things" and was no longer trying to learn new skills so she could gain financial independence, Ashley's father cut off personal and financial support to his daughter. Defiant, Ashley mentioned that her father did not understand what is was like to be homeless and that quitting school was the best option for her and her family at the time. Perhaps Ashley's father did not know what was best for Ashley and her family. However, Ashley's father gave her money specifically for tuition and when the money was used for other reasons, Ashley said that her father had felt "cheated and lied to."

Beyond friends and family, some participants also exaggerated or lied about their circumstances to obtain charity from strangers. As a person who has worked and lived around homeless people, I have heard plenty of stories about homeless people who lied about their circumstances to manipulate a stranger into giving them spare change or buying them some food, clothing, or even a night in a hotel. And while conducting this research, I actually caught a participant in a boldfaced lie as he stood on the corner asking drivers for spare change.

In short, Kenneth was interviewed about two weeks before the incident and his background was fairly well known. However, on this particular day, Kenneth was holding a sign that read, "HOMELESS. HAVE SON. PLEASE HELP US. GOD BLESS." Based on his interview two weeks prior, it was my understanding that Kenneth did not have any immediate family, let alone a son whom he had to support. When Kenneth was approached this time, I said, "Kenneth, I didn't know you had a son." Kenneth replied, "Oh, I don't. I just borrowed this sign from Tracy while he's at work." Kenneth's attitude was casual and he remained focused on his panhandling. As this research continued to conduct interviews with other participants it was learned that sign-sharing was fairly common based on people's schedules. In some cases, current homeless people simply inherited signs from former homeless people who found shelter or left town. As a result, unless the person holding the sign actually created the sign, it is reasonable to question the sign's accuracy. And then again, sometimes even the sign's creator just makes stuff up.

While dishonest, when one thinks about the objectives of a panhandler, one begins to realize that the sign's accuracy is actually irrelevant. Instead, like any good salesperson, a panhandler's main concern is whether the sign works. Tiffany used to panhandle with her aforementioned colleagues José Thomas and Prince Riley, but stopped once she decided that she wanted to get sober. For her, it was too tempting to use the money on alcohol. Tiffany said:

> I know panhandling is wrong, but if people are willing to give, I don't know what the big deal is. It's not hurting anyone. What is it hurting for them to panhandle? I mean, if [people] don't want to give you money, they're not going to give you money. I've

known [José] for 13 years now and people hand him money left and right. We sometimes made up to $600 a day on a weekend and most of it went to alcohol. You just got to know the right spots and give people a good line of bull. If they give you money, it's not hurting anyone.

Like most people who find themselves in difficult circumstances, homeless people learn to adapt so that they can survive. For example, telling someone that you need spare change because you are a middle-aged alcoholic does not get you very far. However, Tiffany, Kenneth, Joe, and Philip discussed how panhandlers used key words such as "family," "son," "daughter," "child," "veteran," and "God bless" to earn sympathy regardless of the validity of the terms' contexts or merits. Dishonesty aside, there is a legitimate method to these tactics that should be appreciated for its organization and ingenuity. And while I remain conflicted about the manipulative and deceitful strategies employed by some of the homeless to acquire charitable support from well-meaning citizens, I continually find myself reflecting on the ethnographic work of Conover (1984) and Riis (1890) who remind us of the vast cultural differences between those who are housed and those who are homeless. Therefore, even though I am conflicted about the deceit, I also recognize that my current circumstances allow me regular access to food, clothing, and shelter. Provided more dire circumstances, I may become less conflicted.

Manipulating Homeless Shelters

The final area where manipulation was found and abuse was happening within the homeless community was at the homeless shelter. Like other programs that were being abused, manipulation within homeless shelters should be understood as a result of personal choices *and* systemic shortfalls. Taking note of Olasky's (1992) conclusions, social programs designed to help the homeless are successful when they uphold rigid structure and require clients to contribute to the shelter's operation and maintenance. Conversely, while researching at Good Sam's, it was observed that this specific shelter had lenient standards, unclear policies, and general chaos. In Good Sam's defense, there were a plethora of reasons why such chaos existed. Most notable were the lack of finances that led to staff reductions and a general lack of oversight. Regardless of the reasons, the results were ultimately the same:

139

Less structure created an environment where clients could manipulate the rules without consequence.

To some regard, many of the ways people manipulated the shelter were innocuous. For example, every day there were always a few people who skipped out on completing their daily chore. Most chores were supposed to be completed after each meal, but some people would eat quickly and leave the shelter before the meal was completed so that they would not have to sweep the floors, wash the dishes, wipe the tables, or put away the chairs. Markedly, these residents were not leaving early for work (employed residents received late-night chores such as laundry and cleaning the bathroom). Instead, these residents were leaving early so they could go hang out with friends. Inevitably, another resident would volunteer to complete the chore, but it was bothersome that certain residents were not contributing to the maintenance of the shelter. Effectively, the residents who avoided doing chores were benefitting from the services of the shelter, but were not being asked to change their personal behaviors (see MacDonald, 2000). Systemically, since there were no consequences for their actions, these residents continued to manipulate the daily chore schedule.

People also manipulated the shelter in more serious ways that cost the shelter valuable resources and money. According to Tiffany:

> There was a lady who just passed through here last week with two kids. She was just using the shelter as a hotel. People do that more than [the staff] knows. They'll just call you all when they're driving and give you some sob story and then end up in the shelter for two or three days, but really that lady was on her way to Memphis, Tennessee. And you hear them out at the picnic table talking and you figure it out and they're just going to see a boyfriend or a girlfriend or something like that and they just don't want to spend the money on a hotel.

In this example, manipulating the shelter for a couple nights' of sleep during travel might only cost the shelter an occupied bed, food, and some additional cleaning cost. However, it can cost hundreds of dollars when the shelter decides to help the person with travel expenses. James explains how he and his friend Robert traveled to Florida and back during a winter "10 years ago" for a free six-month vacation. James said:

> Some of these hoboes literally get off a bus or a train and they give [the staff] a story and they end up staying here for a couple of days and then you guys end up giving them a train ticket and then they go back to wherever-the-hell they came from. That's how me and Robert did it. It was a total bullshit story. Hell, you can tell [shelter work-

ers] anything: need to get home, have a job down south, going to rehab. But [shelter workers] are just getting played for free bus tickets.

While traveling to Florida, James and Robert stayed at various homeless shelters along the way until they could find an agency that would give them enough money to pay for the next leg of the trip. James said that they told people they were construction workers heading to Florida to find work during the winter. In reality, they just wanted to spend the winter in Florida. During one night when they could not find a shelter, Robert, a diabetic, allowed his blood sugar to spike so they could stay at the hospital for a few days. With no place to go once discharged, the hospital paid for a cab to drive them 30 minutes to the nearest homeless shelter.

Whereas some travelers inappropriately used homeless shelters as hotels, other people misused homeless shelters as community lounges instead of using them as places to find services. As a shelter intent on helping homeless people transition into a home, Good Sam's policy stated that people were supposed to vacate the shelter's premises every afternoon to look for jobs or meet with social workers. However, a few people regularly ignored these requirements and instead spent the afternoons sleeping in their rooms, watching television, playing video games, playing cards, or smoking out back. While these types of activities are harmless and much could be written about the need for leisurely activities in order to de-stress, this research specifically wants to highlight those individuals who participated in these activities *every day*. As a result, these individuals left the shelter after 30 days with no more resources, job prospects, or abilities to obtain housing. Critical of some of his fellow residents, Michael said:

> Some people here are just concerned with rolling their tobacco and getting a hold of their next tobacco bag because they don't want anything else. I mean, they've got a bed and they've got some food and they've got another shelter to go to after this one because that's what they do. They just travel from shelter to shelter.

While there are no personal qualms with people who choose to live this type of lifestyle, there are two main points of concern for larger public policy. First, there is a concern that some people might be making these choices by default because they are unaware of how the shelter can help them obtain housing. If this is the case, then the shelter needs to do a better job promoting structure, job skills, and benefit opportunities. Second, for those people who are voluntarily choosing to "travel from shelter to shelter," there is a concern about how organizations are allocating finite resources. In short, should homeless shelters subsidize people who actively choose not to support themselves (see Schiff, 1990) at the expense of allocating fewer resources to people who are trying to support themselves? To this question, shelters might consider instituting more rigorous community standards in order to create an environment where all clients must actively pursue education, work, and housing or face eviction.

During this research, these kinds of policy changes were anything but hypothetical and were rigorously discussed among some staff members at Good Sam's. For example, during one particularly heated rant, the staff supervisor, Tony, said that the shelter's social worker responsible for overseeing intake was too nice and allowed too many people to overstay their 30-day limit. In her defense, Maria's policy was to let people overstay their 30-day limit when they could demonstrate that they were actively securing a job or housing and only "needed a few more days" to finalize. However, Tony's argument was that people were getting "too comfortable" at the shelter and that providing exceptions to any person meant that the shelter had to provide exceptions to every person. As evidence would show, there seemed to be validity for Tony's argument. When this research first started, the daily "resident log" listed about three out of twenty-five residents staying at the shelter for longer than 30 days. Within three months, this number had climbed to nearly half of the residents staying longer than 30 days. A few residents had even been allowed to stay longer than 60 days; far beyond the "few more days" exception. Again, these examples point to breakdowns at both the personal and systemic levels.

Of course, this breakdown in policy did not go unnoticed by residents. Discussing how residents stayed beyond the 30-day limit, Brandon said:

> I haven't seen one [resident] yet leave on their own. Like you just get here one day and leave when you want I guess. Most people aren't really worried about the next step.... As long as you show [Maria] a piece of paper from the county or some application, she'll let you stay as long as you want.

A shelter extension policy that allows residents to turn in paperwork proving their efforts to obtain a job or housing may work with residents who are honest about their efforts and honest with their paperwork. But, according to Michael, this was not always the case:

All I know is that I'm allowed to witness things that [the staff] will never be subjected to because you work here. You know they're not going to tell you the truth. You think I always told the truth to my probation officer? It doesn't take a genius to forge a piece of paper that says, "I looked for a job today." I never looked for no job while I was selling [drugs]. But I had to get the paperwork so I was legit.

When asked about how he would address the loopholes in the policy that allowed some residents to lie about their paperwork, Michael continued:

You just have to be observant. Obviously I've heard people talking when they're outside and there's no staff around and they're free to talk. You have no idea who these people are or what they do to manipulate everybody. I just don't trust them about anything.

While Michael's comments seemed cynical about the ability to trust other residents, it is important to remember that his comments are rooted in personal experiences: first, experiences where he lied about job applications to appease authority and second, experiences where he witnessed others lying about job applications to appease authority. Therefore, while people might debate the extent to which forgery and manipulation happens among the homeless, it is still important to recognize these types of lived experiences as valid and useful when trying to better understand the homeless community as a whole. As Michael made clear during his interview, researchers are outsiders who are not allowed to witness everything that he is allowed to witness. Consequently, there are simply times when researchers have to humble themselves and trust the reported experiences of those who are homeless.

In the end, the root of this research is to embrace the narratives of homeless people as sites of knowledge production. Therefore, communicating narratives about manipulation is just as important as communicating narratives about job loss, home loss, illness, substance abuse, and fractured families. Collectively, all of these experiences provide us a more complete understanding of how homeless people navigate their daily lives. As policymakers continue to create models aimed at ending homelessness, they must be willing to listen to the comfortable *and* the uncomfortable truths. By embracing both the honest and manipulative ways homeless people navigate the culture of homelessness, policymakers become better informed about the culture of homelessness and thus, can create policies that better address these realities.

8. Seeking Recognition/ Finding Community

During the data collection process it was easy to tell when the interview was coming to a close because each participant exhibited the same nonverbal cues: sunken shoulders, eyes focused downward, slowed speech, and a quieting voice just above a whisper. These were the signs of exhaustion. Each participant had just shared his or her story of homelessness and the emotional toll of sharing that story was visible. Under the breathlessness of these closing minutes, participants spoke more philosophically about the complicated relationships between the homeless and the housed as well as discussed their long-term hopes, dreams, and aspirations. Instead of driving the conversations with specific questions during this portion of the interview, I usually sat back and listened to the participant openly reflect on his or her life. It was as if the participant had to work through this part of the interview alone and was simply thinking out loud about the broader implications of homelessness, home, and his or her sense of belonging.

The most poignant closing remarks came from Kristen. While working at the shelter I had gotten to know Kristen over the course of five weeks before she was approached for an interview. Our relationship was warm and friendly and she expressed no hesitations about a meeting. In fact, her face lit up when asked if we could talk after the shift change at four o'clock in the afternoon. The interview had its predictable ups and downs as Kristen shared her struggles and her joys. However, her final thoughts caught me off-guard and stirred deep emotional conflict. As Kristen talked about her relationship with the shelter staff, she said:

> You know, a little bit of thought goes a long way. And a little bit of compassion. You all don't need to treat us like we're just a part of your job because this is our lives.

144

For you this is a job. You all come here at eight o'clock in the morning and you leave at five, but I'm stuck here 24/7. You know what I mean?

Her tone was not malicious, but calm and composed. The question was rhetorical. Yet, her words were alarming and damning and this initiated an immediate defense of the work being done at the shelter and the research being done on the issue of homelessness. While Kristen's soliloquy was not interrupted, I did stop actively listening to her in that moment and focused internal thoughts toward self-affirmation and research-confirmation. My work was justified!

When finally returning to the audio during the transcription phase, I listened to this portion of Kristen's interview numerous times. Each time I listened I became less defensive and could better hear her critique. Kristen was right and even the most well-intentioned and knowledgeable volunteers, social workers, and academics sometimes fall short of fully embodying the type of care, consideration, and compassion necessary when addressing the issue of homelessness. Continuing to voice her frustration, Kristen mentioned that "no one seems to care that I have a family and I'd like to get back home. I have dreams just like everyone else, but you treat me like I'm just your job." Admittedly, straddling the line between broad shelter policy and individual empathy is difficult. On most days there were simply too many people to manage and too many tasks to complete for any staff member to provide any resident with meaningful and extended personalized attention. It was the job of staff members to make sure that the shelter ran smoothly, not that people's emotions were validated or dreams actualized. Staff members weren't therapists. However, this policy-first approach had clearly upset Kristen and her statements should make us think more deeply about the humanizing effects of individualized recognition and encourage us to be more receptive to Kristen's dreams. More specifically, policymakers should ask, "What are Kristen's dreams?" and "Does our work help her achieve her dreams?"

As discussed throughout this research, those who are marginalized are often at the mercy of those who have power (see Mendoza, 2005; see Moon, 1996). For those who are homeless, their lives are shaped by the policies and influences of the housed. This includes everyone from very powerful politicians who shape welfare programs to less powerful shelter workers who shape chore schedules and dictate bedtimes. While these policies may come from a desire to end homelessness, Kristen's remarks remind us that listening to the desires of the homeless should be an important factor in this process. After all, the homeless are the people whose lives are most affected by these policies. Without recognizing the dreams of those who are homeless, policymakers might craft policy that is out of sync with homeless people's ambitions and thus, make it less likely that a homeless person will want to participate in a certain program. Worse yet is the notion that the homeless are made to feel like "projects," as opposed to people, when they are not included in policy discussion. In the end, even if certain policies remain unchanged, making sure that the goals and desires of the homeless have been heard can still help to create a sense of ownership, empowerment, inclusion, and community.

With these ideas in mind, this final chapter of analysis is specifically concerned with how the participants articulate their aspirations as well as how they create a sense of belonging with other homeless people. First, this chapter discusses how the participants are seeking recognition from the housed population. Second, it emphasizes how the participants are searching for stability by entering rehab, reuniting with family, and looking for work. Finally, it highlights how the participants are finding community with other people who are homeless. By better understanding the aspirations of the homeless, the hope is that this chapter will provide some insight about how to build stronger intercultural relationships between the homeless and the housed as well as how to work together to forge policies that can better help the homeless reach their goals while validating their humanity and cultivating a sense of community.

Seeking Recognition

Quite frankly, most of the time the participants felt like no one cared about them or their situations. These feelings are in line with DePastino's (2003) observation that homeless people are not recognized by the larger culture because the homeless have no tangible space of belonging. The homeless have no land, no house, and very little property. These materials are symbolic of a person's establishment, usefulness, and contributions in society. Without these items, people are relegated as less important and prone to becoming invisible. In this

146

study, the most jarring example of how the homeless became invisible was offered by Tiffany. When speaking about the need for southern Illinois to address the increasing homeless population, Tiffany said:

> I thought they were going to do something when they had it on the news about the homeless guy who was found dead on that porch next to the laundry mat a few months ago. And then [the news coverage] was all that happened! People quit talking about it the next day! They just don't care! They don't give a shit! They don't!

Tiffany was speaking fast and shouting. She was using this moment to indict both the callousness and indifference of southern Illinois residents. She continued her tirade by explaining the complicated matrix that sometimes prohibited homeless people from accessing shelter. Tiffany said:

> There's a lot of homeless people right now who can't even come into Good Sam's or go to The Lighthouse or Herrin and they're just basically in the weather all the time and it's just not fair. I can understand banning them if they're die-hard criminals or if there's alcohol or drugs, but there's got to be a different way. You can't just let people freeze to death on the streets.

For Tiffany, the death of this man was personal because she identified with his situation. She may have been expressing anger on his behalf, but her comments were also prompted by the general lack of recognition she had felt on a daily basis. His death represented her invisibility as a homeless person in southern Illinois. She finished this part of the interview by bringing attention to her own story. Tiffany concluded:

> The community needs to open their eyes up to the homeless. We're not all bad people. People lose their jobs. The community automatically thinks that if you're homeless it's drug-related or alcohol-related and it's not. It's loss of jobs. It is. Darren [her husband] lost his job. We had our own place that was $500 every month. Now it's gone. And when you don't have anything everybody acts like you don't matter anymore. It's hard.

Even though she felt invisible, Tiffany refused to give up and even discussed her long-term goal of giving back by helping the homeless. Because she was living through homelessness, Tiffany felt that she was in a position to best understand what the homeless needed as well as what the larger southern Illinois community needed to understand about the homeless. Once she and Darren got a house, Tiffany planned on being more active with the city government and also joked that if she won the lottery, she was "going to build a big-ass homeless shelter" so that no one had to sleep outside anymore.

While recognizing the presence of the homeless through government policy, news media, and community awareness seems like a positive step toward helping the homeless, some participants pointed out the unintended consequences of increased attention. As discussed by Ashley when recalling her story about panhandling, "Once the cops know where you are, they might stop by five or six times a day and tell you to move." Ashley's husband Philip shared a similar hesitation about public exposure as he discussed his family's appearance on a local news network. The news story was intended to be a human interest piece about homeless families in southern Illinois. While Philip originally embraced the interview as a chance to bring attention to the plight of homeless families in general and his family in particular, he was not pleased with the final version of the story. Philip said:

> You know the [news] had us portrayed as bad people because they left out so much stuff. And after doing that interview, that led to us getting kicked out over at the [motel] because of the bad publicity. [The motel] didn't want to be associated with us living there. The public was really nice to us before all of that and we really appreciate what [the public was] doing, but when the news came out [the news] switched [our story] all around like we were just out here to scam people.

The alleged "scam" Philip was discussing was the fact that he and his wife sometimes had their four-year-old daughter with them when they panhandled. According to Philip, she was only with them when other family members could not babysit her and Philip "couldn't very much leave her alone in a hotel room all day." Essentially, she was with her parents all day like any other four-year-old would be with his or her parents all day. However, Philip said the news sensationalized his family's story and made it sound like he and his wife were "using her to get sympathy" from the public.

In addition to sensationalizing their story, Philip was also upset that the news made him look ungrateful. When discussing the story's omissions, Philip said:

> The news just put what they wanted out there and they didn't put anything about us thanking the public or anything like that or anything about our gratitude. You know I'm very grateful to the public because I used to be the person in the car driving by and helping people. So I know what it takes to help a stranger.

To Philip, communicating appreciation was important because it created a bond between him and the public. As Philip put it, "You have to say 'thank you' because we're all in this together." Philip's gratitude was his way of recognizing the public for recognizing and supporting his family. The relationship was supposed to be reciprocal as a means of strengthening the bond, but since the news edited out his "thank you," Philip felt like the news was responsible for weakening his family's relationship with the public. Philip's story demonstrates the difficult choices some homeless people face when seeking recognition. In one regard, it might be a good idea to use the media to highlight homelessness within one's community. However, as Philip learned, once you agree to make your story public, you do not always know how it will be edited and interpreted. Therefore, it was not solely recognition that Philip sought on behalf of homeless families, but recognition that challenged negative stereotypes. Unfortunately, one story with unfavorable editing may actually reinforce those negative stereotypes and create an even wider relational chasm between the homeless and the housed.

Of course negative interpretations of public stories like Philip's have broader implications for other members of the homeless community as well. For example, as Kenneth discussed the negative stereotypes associated with homeless people, he mentioned that some people go out of their way just to shout insults at him. In response to these individuals, Kenneth said:

> The heartless people are difficult. If you don't want to give me anything, then don't give me anything. You don't have to holler at me. Just go about your own life. Don't worry about me like you basically don't anyway.

Like previous examples, this once again shows the difficult terrain that is navigated by the homeless when they make their presence known. Kenneth clearly wanted to be recognized by the public because he was standing on a public corner with a sign asking people for assistance. However, when confronted with negative recognition Kenneth mentioned that people should "just go about" their own lives and not worry about him.

The broader implications of both Philip's and Kenneth's stories are their lack of control over personal narratives. Each man wanted recognition where he could have greater control over both content and context. For homeless people who are already vulnerable to negative stereotypes, ignorance, and invisibility (see Smiley & West, 2012; see Wasserman & Clair, 2010), the ability to control one's public image is increasingly important. However, controlling one's image may prove difficult since housed people are more likely to get their information about homelessness from government officials, medical professionals, or local news stories rather than speaking directly with a homeless person (see Campbell & Reeves, 1989).

Ultimately, Kristen said that homeless people do not want any special treatment and that they are tired of being looked down upon all the time. They just want to be recognized "as any other normal person in your neighborhood" who happens to be going through a "rough spot at the moment." There is no need to demonize, sensationalize, or even lionize their experiences. Homeless people simply want to be treated like people. Grabbing my hand on top of the picnic bench, Kristen humorously reaffirmed this when she closed our conversation with, "You tell 'em that it's okay to talk to us. We won't bite."

Searching for Stability

The invisibility participants felt was simply one more layer that made homelessness mentally and emotionally difficult. Beyond the physical challenges of finding work, income, and housing, homelessness was also described as a state of mind. For example, while fighting for physical survival, participants also fought for affirmation, sobriety, and family relationships. Even though many of their situations were dire, participants discussed the need to focus on their short-term and long-term goals and, according to Maddy, "just get out of the bed every morning and pound the pavement." These mental and emotional struggles often determined participants' optimism, and a steadfast focus on their aspirations provided participants hope for the future. While income and housing gave participants a solid financial foundation for survival, many said that successfully conquering their mental and emotional tribulations is what would truly give them a sense of stability.

One of the first major struggles some participants discussed was alcohol and/or drug abuse. Notably, substance abuse among these participants was a complicated subject because sometimes the abuse led to homelessness and other times the abuse began as a way to cope with homelessness. Whatever the case may have been, each participant who struggled with substance abuse understood sobriety as an important step in their journey out of homelessness. At the time of the interviews, three participants admitted to regularly using alcohol or drugs and were self-described addicts. Two additional participants had previously been addicts and were now sober, but would "always struggle with this demon." One current user, James, indicted that he "wishes" to be sober and described his current alcohol abuse as the "last big hurdle." James said:

> Oh, I can [work], but no one wants to hire me because of my drug charge. And since I can't work, I drink. I can't get a job anyway. It's just back-and-forth. Maybe if I could stay sober for six months or a year and have some caseworker vouch for me, then an employer might say, "Well all that's in the past, so we'll hire you." But who wants to stay sober when you have to live out here. Hell, I couldn't live out here if I didn't drink [laughs].

Like James, other participants described the temptation of alcohol and/or drugs and the impact it had on their ability to find financial, mental, and emotional stability. While she had been sober for more than five years at the time of our interview, Maddy still attended Alcoholics Anonymous and Narcotic Anonymous meetings at least once a week. For Maddy, attending these meetings was necessary so she could remind herself never to abuse alcohol or drugs again. However, these meetings also reminded her of her past and each time she went it was "like a reminder of how [she] messed up [her] life." Maddy continued:

> I mean, I want a normal home life like everybody else, which sounds kind of stupid because I don't even know what a "normal home" is. It just sucks because I made stupid mistakes with drugs when I was younger and I'm still paying for it and I'll always be paying for it because I have to go to these meetings all the time. Going to A.A. isn't "normal."

For Maddy, going to these meetings was a choice. She was not under any sort of court order or parole obligation. Her attendance was completely voluntary and put her in a bind. If she did not attend, she worried that she would relapse. Yet, her attendance made her feel like she was still an addict and incapable of living a normal life. She had not yet figured out how to be at peace with this paradox and until she could, she worried that she would never "be happy."

In addition to sobriety, participants also wanted to reestablish relationships with family members. By healing family relationships, participants hoped that they would be afforded a fresh start. Much like Maddy's description of alcohol and drug abuse, lingering family friction reminded participants of their past lives and many believed that they could not move forward with their lives until they had made amends. In one example, Tiffany said that nothing would feel more like "home" than having her son back in her life. However, about two years ago, Tiffany and her son had an argument over him losing his job. Tiffany said:

I blew up at him because he had a career with the Army National Guard and he wouldn't listen to them and he messed up real bad and got kicked out. So I got real mad at him for screwing up his life and some words were exchanged and that was it. And he's homeless like we are now and I don't want to see him homeless.

Tiffany's son still lives around the southern Illinois area and she sees him "every once in a while." However, they never speak to one another because "he's never forgiven" her for some of the things she said about him. Tiffany would not say what she had said to her son because she couldn't bring herself to "repeat those awful things." If Tiffany had to choose, she said she would rather have a relationship with her son and live on the streets than get an apartment right now because an apartment "is a building" whereas her son makes her feel like she "is home."

Finally, participants talked about finding stability in work. For many, work was not only about the money, but about helping them feel like productive members of society. According to Brandon, "Work just makes you feel good." After spending time in jail, Brandon said he waits for the day when he "can have a normal job like a normal person." He continued:

> I just want to get all of these fines paid off, get off parole, and stay out of trouble. I'm gonna get me a job and just stay with my family and work. That's my main goal. I don't want to be no CEO of no company or anything special like that. I don't need to be rich or nothing. I just want to have a regular job so I can see my family and maybe they'll finally be proud of me [laughs].

Brandon's remarks about his family "finally being proud" were in reference to his lengthy criminal past. In addition to financial stability, work was Brandon's way of turning a corner and creating a new life for himself. The importance of steady work was its ability to prove to Brandon that he could have the life he imagined. Instead of being a criminal, he could be a family man. Instead of always taking from society, work provided him a means of giving back. And with any luck, work would bring him peace.

Finding Community

The compounded search for work, family, and stability coupled with the lack of humanizing public recognition caused many of the participants to express feelings of intense loneliness and desperation. To help alleviate some of these feelings the participants formed small groups or partnerships. While these partnerships were no substitute for family, there was reassurance in knowing that many participants had a supportive community that was willing to stand by them while they navigated homelessness. In addition to camaraderie and empathy, these interpersonal relationships also served a practical function. Mainly, because the possibility of becoming homeless is so foreign to many people, few people ever prepare for the day when they may have to live on the streets. Therefore, living in community with other homeless people was a way to share knowledge, resources, and burdens.

Joe remembers his first few weeks living on the streets and how thankful he was to have Kenneth by his side. When Joe became homeless, Kenneth had already been living on the streets for four years and had cultivated a lot of practical experience. Joe said:

> This is my first time being on the streets. When you're 34 and never been homeless before you really don't see it happening to you. [Before you become homeless] you think, "Well I made it this far in life without any real problems so I'll be fine." But when you get out here you have no freakin' idea what to do. But luckily I had [Kenneth] and he's helped me with some of the ins and outs. He really showed me the ropes; like dealing with all the people. I've never been much dealing with new people, but he helped me go to this welfare office and this church and now I'm out here asking people for money. So he really helped me in that way so I can interact with people now because you have to [interact with people] so much.

Joe felt fortunate to have found a partnership with someone as experienced as Kenneth who could help him with the daily tasks of navigating homelessness. However, practical experience is not the only characteristic these types of partnerships bring. These partnerships also bring solace and the comfort of knowing that someone else understands your situation and your burdens. These were the kinds of sentiments expressed by Tiffany when she spoke about her relationship with her husband Darren.

At the time of her interview, Tiffany had been homeless, on and off, for four years. When she first became homeless she was in a relationship with a man named Dominic. In the following passage, she describes the difference between being homeless with Dominic and being homeless with Darren. Tiffany said:

> Homelessness is a lot to take in. I mean, it's easier having someone going through it with you who is committed to getting out. With [Dominic], he didn't want to work.

He didn't even want to work at getting work. So it was like I was pulling weight for two people and at the time I had no idea what I was doing. So I was kind of figuring it all out by myself. With [Darren], he had a job he lost because of my surgery, but we pulled together and we're working on getting out together. I don't think I could make it alone. I don't think anyone can make it out here alone. With [Dominic], I was pretty much alone anyway and it wasn't working. I don't feel alone with [Darren]. We'll get out.

According to Tiffany, Darren lost his job because she had surgery and his company was not willing to pay for the increasing price of his health insurance. While Tiffany was literally in the same financial and housing situation with Darren as she was with Dominic, her attitude and outlook were different. Whereas Tiffany and Dominic clashed over expectations and work ethic, Tiffany and Darren shared the same expectations regarding how they could work together to find stable housing and stable income. Sharing these goals with Darren provided Tiffany hope and relieved her of some emotional angst. Instead of Tiffany navigating homelessness alone, Darren was willing to carry part of that stressful burden.

To be sure, not every working relationship within the homeless community was as amiable as Tiffany and Darren's relationship. Instead, like most communities, the participants in this study had interpersonal conflicts with other homeless people whom they needed to interact with on a daily basis in order to survive. The most colorful story encountered during this research illustrating how some participants negotiated community standards involved ongoing tensions between Joe, Kenneth, Philip, and Ashley. In short, Joe and Kenneth panhandled together at one corner while Philip and Ashley panhandled together at a different corner. When Kenneth described the conflict, he said:

Me and [Philip] were fighting over this corner because it gets the most traffic. The way I think it should go is that if you want the corner—and I told him this—then I said, "If you want the corner, then get your lazy ass out the damn bed and get the corner!" But his wife [Ashley] was trying to crowd me off the corner and said it was unfair that I only got the good corner 'cause I sleep right over there.

During her interview, Ashley discussed her perspective on the situation. Ashley said:

You know, I'm a big girl and I can't walk very far or very fast. So I always tried to take that corner and I'd sometimes wake up at 6:30 in the morning just to beat [Kenneth] there, but I could never get there fast enough. And we had some pushing wars and stuff and finally we all just sat down and said, "Hey, this is crazy. There's plenty of corners out here for everyone." So we started switching days. "You out there one day and we're there the next day." Now it's pretty cool and everybody gets along.

For his part, Philip claimed to be the person who came up with the schedule. When discussing his role in the agreement, Philip said:

> Now we work together. And when new people come out here we kind of show them what territory they can have. You know, because people used to call the police on me and [Kenneth] when we was out there arguing. But it ain't worth all that attention 'cause it gives the wrong impression to the people about who we are and what we're about. We had our little turf war, but we had to come to an agreement because if we fought all the time, then no one gets nothing. I mean, you don't have to like everybody out here, but you have to learn to help each other out and watch each other's back because we're all out here struggling.

The two partnerships still bickered about the corners, but each recognized the need to resolve the conflict in a way that would be beneficial to everyone. Furthermore, each partnership recognized that their individual reputations were tied to the public's overall perception of the homeless community. According to Joe:

> Some of the people I've met out here I wouldn't have even thought twice about associating with because I thought I was better than them. But [Philip and Ashley] actually turned my outlook on things completely around because I saw that we were all in the same boat. Do I like them? No. But we all kind of have to get along because we're all kind of doing the same job, if that makes sense.

Joe began to recognize that he was part of a homeless community and that the actions of one member within that community reflected on the community as a whole. Furthermore, Joe explained that his success on the corners was intrinsically linked to Philip and Ashley's success because most drivers viewed all panhandlers the same way. Therefore, it was in his best interest to work with other homeless people (even those he did not care for) so that the entire community could benefit.

This situation is just one example where homeless people came together to solve problems that were unique to the homeless experience. These types of unique experiences created community standards and bonded homeless people together in a way that distinguished the culture of homelessness from the culture of the housed population (see Ravenhill, 2008). These bonds were also present at the shelter where community members regularly leaned on one another for resources, strength, and support. As reiterated by several participants, working together was inevitable because "We're all in this together." This recognition of shared struggle and shared objectives (mainly, working their ways out of homelessness) was what opened the doors for endless acts of selflessness and hospitality between complete strangers. For example, at Good Sam's, experienced clients regularly clamor around new residents to take them on tours, explain the rules, teach them how to properly complete chores, and show them the information board, which provided information about jobs, government assistance, and bus schedules. Residents like Christina, who had a physical disability, regularly received help from strangers who carried her and her wheelchair up and down the stairs when the wheelchair lift broke.

On the streets, participants talked about always sharing their knowledge of panhandling with new people. Even though new panhandlers created increased competition for drivers' spare change, Joe, Kenneth, Philip, and Ashley each shared stories about helping people get started. Joe said:

> There was this new kid out here just a few days ago doing it all wrong. So I went up to him and gave him a little advice and said, "Look, if you want to make any money this is how you do it." And I showed him. "Don't sit on your ass. Don't make yourself look comfortable. People don't like that. They think you're lazy and you don't want to do nothing. And make you a bigger sign. Darken the words. And put a shirt on. Cover up all those tattoos." You know, just trying to help him look presentable where he doesn't offend people.

Again, Joe's actions demonstrated a connection among homeless people that reinforced their shared community and indicated that Joe understood "this new kid's" struggles. Joe was teaching "this new kid" lessons much like Kenneth had taught Joe when Joe first started living on the streets. Perhaps, "this new kid" would someday pass these lessons on to someone else.

In the end, the help and guidance that happens among homeless people reinforce the ideas of shared struggle and shared community. Furthermore, the type of help and guidance are unique to the homeless community because the challenges the homeless community faces are unique. When asked why homeless people go out of their way to help one another, Brandon said:

> Sometime there're people at Good Sam's who are acting like they're more worse off than anybody, but they're not. I mean, there's people that get depressed, but everybody talks to them and tells them, "Hey, just forget it. Don't worry about it." We kind

of talk them up and tell them, "Hey, it's no big deal. We're all going through it too and we'll help you out."

While Brandon does not offer any tangible solutions for a person trying to escape homelessness, loneliness, or depression, he does let people know that they belong to a community of people who understand the distinctive challenges that come with being homeless. Moreover, Brandon validates and empathizes with their emotions. This is not the type of validation and empathy that can be given by a social worker, a benevolent politician, or even a loving family member because none of these individuals "are going through it." This type of empathetic support can only be given by someone who is homeless: someone who resides in the homeless community and experiences the same emotional difficulties, doubts, and vulnerabilities every day.

PART IV
WHAT'S NEXT?

9. Conclusion

Perhaps the most significant methodological accomplishment of this research was that it centered homeless people's voices. In most research and public policy, the voices of the homeless are ignored and therefore, many politicians and scholars are failing to capitalize on the wealth of knowledge that resides within the voices and experiences of homeless people. Consequently, most public policy is crafted from the vantage point of those who are housed and financially stable, while personal insights from those who lack adequate housing and/or who are hurting financially are marginalized (see hooks, 2000). This can lead to the creation of policies and programs that fail, not because politicians and scholars are depraved, but because politicians and scholars are not in touch with the cultural differences of those who use social welfare programs (Murray, 2012). In an attempt to interrupt the pattern of politically-driven policies that have generated poor results, this research intentionally leaned on the experiences and the narratives of the homeless in an effort to better understand how the homeless moved through the world. By doing so, this research gathered a wealth of knowledge from those who are homeless and made it possible to use this data to envision policies and programs that are driven from the experiences of the homeless, instead of driven by the theories of the scholars.

In addition to gathering knowledge that can be useful in creating better-functioning policies for the homeless, this study also highlighted the importance of creating communities that are emotionally supportive and respectful of the homeless. While knowing how the homeless use food stamps, unemployment benefits, shelters, and transportation is practically important for creating better policy, listening to the difficult stories about personal turmoil, sense of loss, and abject desperation can be emotionally important for everyday support. Too often housed people make assumptions about the homeless regarding addiction, criminal behavior, and laziness (Smiley & West, 2012; Wasserman & Clair, 2010). As many participants stated, they were tired of being pre-judged by housed people who did not, or would not, take the time to learn about their experiences. As Joe remarked, "At least know my situation before you judge me." By engaging in conversation with the homeless, this research attempted to offer respect for the participants' viewpoints and insights. Instead of assuming what the participants needed (or needed to be lectured on), this research took the time to ask and listen. I have no grand illusions that these short conversations with each participant somehow "solved the problem" or made me more enlightened about the issue of homelessness. However, upon completing this research, it is even more convincing that narrative-centered research is important because it showcases the human aspects of homelessness through the voices of the homeless, and it creates a medium for the homeless to dialogue with the housed in a world that oftentimes ignores their voices.

These intentional dialogues (both formal and informal) between the homeless and this researcher created the circumstances where both parties could experience growth and change. For example, over the last decade I have gained an enormous amount of knowledge about how homeless people manage their lives in Camden, New Jersey, southern Illinois, and numerous communities in between. As an academic interested in proposing public policies, this information helps inform political opinions and policy suggestions. For the participants, dialogue can be an important tool on the journey toward empowerment (see Montalbano-Phelps, 2004). Through the interview process, participants were allowed to "talk back" to caseworkers, shelter staff, politicians, former employers, the media, and the public. While speaking within the confines of a dyadic interview may have been a feeble outlet for some of the anger and frustration directed toward others, the storytelling process can act as an empowering exercise where participants give voice to their experiences as a way to make sense of the current situation (Montalbano-Phelps, 2004). During the formal aspects of this study, questions were posed that asked participants to reflect on their experiences. In doing so, participants discussed how they became homeless, how they moved through homelessness, and their goals for surviving and/or escaping homelessness. While articulating these experiences does not guarantee that a person will escape homelessness, articulating these experiences can create a sense of ownership over them and interpersonal dialogues can help make sense of them.

Reflecting on the intimate dialogues had during this research leads to recognizing another important methodological accomplishment of the study that is applicable to all narrative-based research. Mainly, relationships matter. More specifically, relationships between scholars and participants matter. Fostering a healthy relationship between researchers and participants is important because of the genuine personal differences that exist. For example, I had a house, I had an income, I initiated the conversation, and I asked the questions. While I did my best to engage in power-neutral dialogue, the truth is that social conditions created an imbalance of power that could not be erased. In my mind, this complicated issues of trust and mistrust and brought forth concerns about how much knowledge I could actually glean from the participants. If information was withheld because the participants did not trust me, how accurate was my retelling? My struggle with this unshakable imbalance is shared and captured by other scholars. Of his *five-year* ethnographic work among the poor and homeless, Duneier (2001) wrote,

> ...there were times when the trust I thought I had developed was nothing more than an illusion: deep suspicion lingered despite an appearance of trust. In some cases, perhaps it always will. Surely it takes more than goodwill to transcend distrust that comes out of a complex history [p. 14].

Notably, Duneier's words do not mean that scholars should disengage with vulnerable and marginalized populations. Instead, his words remind scholars that we have a responsibility to constantly and consistently engage in relationship building and maintenance in order to earn participants' trust. If scholars want to learn about homelessness from those who are homeless, then we need to recognize the power that comes with our class standing and understand the skepticism this might cause for those who are homeless and/or financially unstable (see Campbell & Reeves, 1989; see Whiting, 1971).

Finally, the last accomplishment of this study specific to future academic research was that it further solidified earlier assertions that homelessness should be studied from within the field of intercultural communication. Like Daniel (1970), Whiting (1971), and Philipsen (1976), this research indicates that class status is an important cultural distinction. Moreover, it should be added that housing status also increases the cultural differences between socio-economic classes. To

161

be clear, this does not contend that people who are homeless have drastically different wants, needs, and desires compared to those who are housed. On the contrary, the homeless and the housed share many of the same long-term goals. However, the ways the homeless move through the world embodies a culture and a lifestyle that many people could never imagine. This makes the culture of homelessness unique and worth studying within intercultural communication.

For instance, there is little sense of permanency in the culture of homelessness, and the homeless must adapt to new circumstances every day. When the participants of this study woke up each morning, they did not always know where they would sleep that night, what they would eat during the day, or with whom they would interact. Saving money was seldom an option and some participants spent hours gathering change just to buy a sandwich, or if they were lucky, a hotel room for the night. Furthermore, gathering resources sometimes meant blurring the lines between legal and illicit activity. For instance, people trading food stamps, cheating unemployment benefits, or lying when panhandling was socially acceptable within the homeless community and many homeless people talked openly about this type of behavior.

The culture of homelessness also maintains social norms that deprive members of personal privacy and limit agency. For the most part, the homeless live a very public lifestyle. They live in public, sleep in public, eat in public, use the restroom in public, and continuously interact with the public for resources. While housed people also move through public spaces, there are two key differences in the interaction. First, housed people have the choice of returning to private space. Second, housed people are often welcomed in public spaces because it often means they are purchasing goods and services. On the other hand, the homeless are often castigated in public spaces for making paying customers uncomfortable.

Additionally, many homeless people seeking public help must submit all their private information to caseworkers and government employees. This type of vulnerable exposure would make most people uncomfortable, notwithstanding the embarrassment of telling a stranger you are homeless. Regarding agency, most of the participants' days were dictated by other people, such as shelter staff, caseworkers, and government employees. These individuals told the participants when to wake up, when to eat, where to go, what to do, and when to go to bed. For those of us with homes, it is hard to imagine the lack of privacy and limited agency that comes with having your daily actions exposed and controlled by others. For these reasons, various social science disciplines should expand their ideas about culture, cultural criticism, and intercultural communication in order to support intercultural research that is more inclusive of class and housing differences. By positioning homelessness as a distinct culture, scholars are better positioned to explore the unique cultural differences and challenges of homelessness. Recognizing these differences will also allow scholars to explore innovative solutions best fitted for confronting these unique cultural challenges.

Implications for Policy Changes

In writing about government policies aimed at helping the poor, economist Walter Williams (2011) states, "Decent people promote policy in the name of helping the poor and disadvantaged. Those policies can make their ostensible beneficiaries worse off, because policy is often evaluated in terms of intentions rather than effects.... Compassionate policy requires dispassionate analysis. Policy intentions and policy effects often bear no relationship to one another" (p. 3).

Before diving into recommendations for policy changes, it is important to take a moment to draw attention to the first two words of this passage: "Decent people." As a scholar engaged in the debate over social welfare programs, I recognize the hard work and genuine care of politicians and scholars who devote their time to finding solutions to various social problems. Therefore, it is not my intention, nor do I believe that it should be anyone else's intention, to demonize politicians and scholars who devote their time to solving these issues, yet happen to come up with conclusions that some find objectionable. The intention of this research is to follow the data as presented and to come up with recommendations that will be most beneficial in fostering positive results. Others may reach different conclusions, but I trust that they are simply following the data they have been given. I only ask for the same generosity.

With that, this study gathered data that drew attention to the challenges homeless people faced and lifestyles they lived. In doing so, the participants of this study provided a wealth of knowledge about how they lived, worked, ate, and slept. This knowledge directs us toward concrete implications that should be considered when crafting future policies that address homelessness. This research does not claim that these suggestions will yield positive results for every homeless person in every circumstance in every community. However, based on the current dismal trends in successfully housing the homeless, I strongly feel that we need new and creative policies for addressing homelessness and that these policies should be driven by the narratives of the homeless. The hope is that the following suggestions offered for public policy, shelter policy, and the housed community will be taken seriously among the conversations currently happening about how local, state, and federal governments might better address homelessness in our communities.

Implications for Public Policy

The first implication for public policy is one that has been advocated for since the conception of this research: Homeless people should have a voice in crafting public policy. By listening to the voices of the homeless, policymakers will have a better understanding about the culture of homelessness and, therefore, a better understanding about how homeless people use public benefits. This is why this research also supports giving local communities more control over benefit distribution. Currently, state and federal officials are mostly in charge of benefit distribution and rarely interact with those who receive benefits. In response to this dated and ineffective model, this research suggests that local communities be given the money currently allocated for state and federal benefits on the condition that local policymakers reach out to the homeless in their community and thoughtfully discuss with them city budgets, the shelter system, job placement, and benefit distribution. By including homeless people in these discussions, local policymakers strengthen their relationships with the homeless and the homeless get a voice in determining how local benefits are distributed. Most importantly, local policymakers can better respond to the needs of the homeless in their community compared to the uninformed and impersonal responses from state capitals or Washington, D.C. This isn't to say that state and federal government officials are incapable of caring for the homeless; only that it is impossible for distant government officials to understand and manage the specific needs of the tens-of-thousands of diverse communities within the United States.

For example, if southern Illinois policymakers knew how hard it was for the homeless to effectively use food stamps, then local policymakers may consider not allowing homeless people to obtain food stamps from the local governments and instead choose to invest that money into soup kitchens and shelters. Unlike individual homeless people, soup kitchens and shelters can buy in bulk and refrigerate. This would also make it easier and more affordable for homeless people to consume fresh produce and nutritious meals since soup kitchens and shelters would now have more financial resources. Once a homeless person secured a living arrangement and could verify his or her address, food stamp benefits would be reinstated. On the surface it seems counterintuitive (and cruel) to take food stamps away from homeless people. However, if we want to create a system where homeless people have access to nutritious meals and, collectively, we are only willing to spend a limited amount of public money on food security for the poor, then this idea is worth considering. In the end, this type of system would provide much better food options for the homeless in southern Illinois if shelters were given more money to provide healthy food in bulk, as opposed to each homeless person having to buy expensive pre-packaged meals at convenience stores.

Now this idea may not work in every community because not every community has a shelter or a soup kitchen. For some homeless people, food stamps may be the only way they can obtain food. However, if local communities are given the money and allowed to budget the benefits to their community's needs, then decisions over food security, housing, and job placement programs can all be made at the local level in conversation with the local homeless population. These individualized decisions simply cannot happen at a state or federal level because each local community's homeless population has such different needs. Of course, the state and federal government would provide oversight to ensure that *all the money* given to a local government for the homeless was being allocated for the homeless. That being said, there is a finite amount of government resources allocated to address homelessness and it is important to use those resources wisely. By taking a local approach that includes the voices of the homeless in city budget discussions, relationships are made stronger at the local level and the homeless are given the power to help decide how local resources are allocated. Succinctly, people who are homeless can attend, speak at, and contribute to city council meetings in ways that are impossible on the state and federal level.

Finally, when it comes to public policy, this research agrees with other scholars who have previously concluded that receiving public benefits should be contingent on work requirements (see Lundahl & Wicks, 2010; see Olasky, 1992; see Shipler, 2005). Those who oppose linking benefits to work requirements may accuse me of advocating this idea because I think the homeless are "lazy" and the only way to get them to work is by holding their benefits hostage. I do not think this at all. During the past decade of working and volunteering in homeless communities, I have witnessed homeless people who woke up early, panhandled all day, walked 10 miles to a job interview, performed manual labor, and volunteered around shelters. I know that most homeless people are willing to work. Therefore, linking benefits to work requirements is not advocated because the homeless are "lazy." Instead, linking benefits to work requirements is advocated so the homeless can maintain job skills and avoid lengthy gaps in work history.

Of course the difficulty with implementing a work requirement is opportunity. Therefore, it is suggested that these opportunities come through local government departments. Moreover, if a person is already receiving local government benefits, then it makes sense that he or she should contribute to the local government's daily functions. For example, in exchange for $500 per month in combined benefits, a homeless person could be required to perform 50 hours of work per month. As you may recall, a version of this idea was given by Philip in Chapter 6 when he talked about working for the government in exchange for rent money. Some of the jobs people could perform include park maintenance, building maintenance, custodial work, office assistance, or recycling and trash collection. While these entry-level jobs are not the most glamorous, they would promote job skills, fill work history, and provide current references. Of course, this model also encourages accountability on behalf of the beneficiary. In short, if a person does not complete his work hours, then he would temporarily lose benefits. And if the local government is responsible for both benefit distribution and work requirements, then it would be easier to maintain this sort of accountability. In the end, work requirements are an ideal long-term strategy because a person who stays active in the workforce is in a much better position for securing full-time work in the future.

Implications for Shelter Policy

Regarding shelter policy, there are two primary implications that stand out: access and accountability. First, access is an issue that can best be addressed by the shelter staff. As mentioned by several participants, shelter policy can be confusing. There are rules about who can stay, how long a person can stay, and what a person should accomplish while he or she is staying at the shelter. To help streamline these rules and make shelters more accessible, shelters should implement a more generous "open door" policy and allow people to stay for longer than 30 days. For example, there are rules that prohibit some former criminals or addicts from accessing shelter. If shelters prohibit these individuals from accessing shelter based on past behavior, then these individuals remain trapped in homelessness with no initial support. The obvious exception to this policy would be someone with a current warrant. Additionally, the 30-day policy that forces people to leave most southern Illinois shelters after a month is arbitrary and, in some cases, counterproductive. As Brandon summarized, shelters "need to make the time longer so people can get their footing." Otherwise, people tend to move from one shelter to the next without establishing any foundations for long-term success.

Now, access is only one-half of the equation. The other half is accountability, and that must be accomplished by the clients (see Mac-Donald, 2000; see Olasky, 1992; see Schiff, 1990). Currently, a person can enter a southern Illinois shelter, do nothing for 30 days, and then get asked to leave. This helps no one. Therefore, this research proposes that when clients enter a shelter, they set up a plan with a caseworker immediately. Based on a client's skills, needs, and goals, the caseworker would help the client create a plan for achieving certain benchmarks while living at the shelter. This might include enrolling in an educational program, securing a job, saving money, or entering rehab. As long as a person continues to reach these personalized benchmarks on an agreed upon time schedule, he can continue to stay at the shelter.

Yet, if, for example, a caseworker and client agree that the client needs to obtain a formal education and the client fails to enroll in G.E.D. classes by the end of the first week, then the shelter can ask that client to leave immediately. This type of system encourages shelters to give each client a chance as well as allows shelters to hold clients accountable. Of course, things like drug use, violence, or curfew violations can be grounds for immediate dismissal. However, if a person stays clean and is making progress toward financial and living independence, then it does not make any sense to ask him or her to leave after 30 days. This will only work to undercut progress.

Other forms of accountability may include mandatory A.A. meetings or N.A. meetings for former addicts and required work around the shelter, such as cleaning, cooking, construction, and lawn care. Another way that shelters can encourage clients to contribute is by mandating that clients forfeit their food stamp cards to purchase food for the shelter. This helps the shelter with food expenses as well as connects the clients to the overall wellbeing of the shelter. Ultimately, what is encouraging about an access/accountability model is that it requires no additional money or resources. It only requires a policy change that tells clients, "You can stay here as long as you want, as long as you meet personalized benchmarks."

Finally, it is suggested that local shelters share client information with each other. This will help shelter caseworkers figure out who is trying to manipulate the system by moving from one shelter to the next every few weeks. If clients know they can move from one shelter to the next every 30 days with no accountability, then the overall system is not encouraging them to make the necessary changes needed to escape homelessness. Instead, shelters should work together to help create a solid foundation for their clients that encourages clients to invest in long-term strategies for success. By sharing client information, shelters can better assess where people have been, what type of progress they have made, and how to hold them accountable for their actions.

Implications for the Housed Community

While changes to social welfare programs affect government agencies that institute policy and community shelters that provide benefits, this study also encourages greater public awareness for non-homeless community members who interact with the homeless under less formal circumstances. Ultimately, both the homeless and the housed benefit when the housed community is better educated about homelessness and the local resources available in their community. For instance, if shelters adopt more "open door" policies and allow clients to stay as long as they need (provided that the client is making progress), then the local community needs to be aware of these policies. This would help accomplish two things.

First, the housed community members who interact with the homeless would be able to provide this information to the homeless people they encounter. For example, if a homeless person is new to the area and needs help securing food and shelter, then a housed person could inform the homeless person where these resources are available. If the homeless person acts on the information, then the homeless person accomplished his objective of securing food and shelter. This information also puts the person in contact with caseworkers and volunteers who have additional resources that can help him reach long-term objectives such as housing, counseling, or job placement.

Second, education about local resources provides the housed community with the confidence needed to interact with the homeless. Quite frankly, interacting with a homeless person can sometimes be awkward or even intimidating; especially if the homeless person is asking for money or assistance. When strangers approach strangers asking for money, some people may be unsure about how to respond. I know that when I started working with the homeless I was uncertain about how to respond to money questions. I thought about things such as, "How much should I give this person?" and "Does this person really need money for food?" However, by educating the housed community about local resources, the housed community has the information needed for creating dialogue about resources, as opposed to feeling pressured to hand over spare change and quickly leaving. For instance, if a person asks me for money to buy food or secure shelter, I know that I can say, "There is a local shelter nearby that will provide you food and shelter for as long as you need." In some instances, I may even offer to drive the person there. When this approach has been used in the past, some people have accepted my offer and some people have rejected it. Either way, knowing information about local resources creates the possibility for having a dialogue about resources, needs, and long-term goals.

Arguably, some may find this approach tasteless and may even argue that questions regarding someone else's financial intentions are "none of my business." These assessments are fair, and to be clear, I am not advocating that every person needs to interact in this way with regard to resources. All that is being proposed is the notion that housed people learn about the available resources and policies in their communities so that they can engage in conversations with the homeless in a way that makes them feel knowledgeable, confident, and comfortable. Some housed people may know that a local shelter has an abundant amount of food and plenty of spare beds, yet still choose to give homeless people money with no required accountability. While I am personally against this approach, it is every person's right to engage in this activity. The only recommendation here is to insist that housed people know what resources are available, where they are available, and how they are available to the homeless community. This way a member of the housed community who is interested in helping the homeless can at least make informed choices about how he or she wishes to allocate personal resources.

Returning to Camden

While I stand firmly behind the aforementioned implications for policy, I recognize that these recommendations were proposed based on the limited scope of this research. In reflecting on the scope of this research, the following section offers insights about the limitations of this research as well as how these limitations might be addressed in future research. I am sure that others will come to different conclusions about the limitations of this research and propose new methods for studying homelessness in future research. I welcome these critiques and remain very interested in learning about how other scholars are approaching research with the homeless. However, reflecting on this research, there are four specific areas where future research might be expanded: number of participants, length of data collection, additional focus on political and shelter operations, and location.

The first limitation of this study was the number of formal participants interviewed. While there were casual conversations with a few dozen homeless people on the streets and in the shelter, the primary points of data analysis were the 10 formal interviews. And herein lies the tension between quantitative and qualitative methods: Quantitative methods can collect data from hundreds, if not thousands, of participants to discover more generalizable conclusions, however, the personal narrative of each participant is restrained. And while I am eternally grateful to the scholars who have been collecting and sifting through numbers for decades, my interest resides in coupling this quantitative data with the personal narratives to create a richer understanding of homelessness.

Ultimately, collecting, analyzing, and publishing more interviews in future research would simply produce more information about how the homeless move through the world. Beyond increased data for analysis, interviewing more people would also serve as an outlet for more homeless people to share their stories. Access to voice is important for any person (Burke, 1968; Fisher, 1984). However, in this particular situation it is important to remember that public policy regarding food, housing, and welfare is constantly being debated and these debates directly impact the lives of the homeless, usually without their input. By interviewing more participants in the future, I hope to produce a sizeable amount of narrative-driven research that will amplify the voices of the homeless and create more room for their opinions within public policy debates.

The second limitation of this study was its length. Due to time and monetary constraints, the data collection process of formal interviews only took place over a period of three months. Future research should expand the data collection process to at least one year for two primary reasons. First, it is assumed that weather conditions affect how the homeless utilize shelters and other charitable services. In the summer months (the period when this data was collected), the homeless have more choices when it comes to shelter. For example, if a person wishes to avoid shelter policies about drug use, drunkenness, or curfew, he or she usually has the option of sleeping outside because the weather conditions are more favorable. However, when the weather conditions are dangerously cold in the winter, then sleeping outside is less of an option. Therefore, it would be prudent to learn about who accesses shelter resources at different times throughout the year and why.

The second reason a longer study should be conducted is simply so participants can offer feedback during the writing process. Unfortunately, this research process was time-sensitive and demanded an approach that kept moving towards a closing date. Future research without such time constraints should attempt to write up the analysis, give the first-draft of the analysis to the participants, and use their feedback to rework the final manuscript. While the participants in this study were provided an opportunity to narrate their lived experiences through the interview process, they were not provided an opportunity in crafting how those narratives would be edited alongside other narratives. More time would mean that researchers and participants could work as co-authors to complete a more participant-centered manuscript.

The third limitation of this study was the limited attention paid to political and shelter operations. In conducting this research, the primary focus was learning about homelessness through the perspectives of the homeless. However, this is only one perspective in a much broader story about how homelessness is managed in our communities. To gather more perspectives about homelessness, future research could interview non-homeless people who deal with homelessness on a daily basis. This might include politicians in charge of budgeting benefits as well as shelter workers who make policy. While I tend to favor listening to the stories of the homeless because their voices have been largely silenced in public debates, I am sympathetic to those politicians and shelter workers who have to create budgets and enforce policies. I may disagree with some of their decisions, but I recognize that making budget and policy decisions is challenging and can involve very complex hierarchies of many people and groups. Furthermore, there are limited resources in these hierarchies and compromises have to be made. Looking at the political process and shelter structure through the voices of these individuals could provide some great insight for better understanding the challenges they face when trying to make and implement new policies and budgets. It would also be interesting to analyze the narratives of shelter employees and government service workers alongside the narratives of the homeless for comparison. By researching homelessness through different perspectives, researchers would find where different groups agree and disagree on certain policy issues, which could lead to figuring out how to create better-functioning policies that are satisfying for all parties.

The final limitation of this study was its location. Not only was this study conducted in a relatively small physical area, but also in a region with specific population demographics. Over time, energy and resources should be used to collect narratives from homeless communities across the globe. I, for one, am primarily interested in performing an immediate follow-up study in an urban environment because an urban environment offers the most salient contrast. Urban environments pose different challenges (e.g., safety, access to drugs) for the homeless community and offer different benefit systems (e.g., more charities, more government funding) that the homeless must navigate. Some future research might look at the size of the urban homeless population and compare whether larger populations of homeless people using shelters and services affect how people narrate loss, privacy, and community. It would also be interesting to listen to the narratives of the urban homeless and compare their needs, wants, and desires to those of the rural homeless. If there are need differences between urban and rural homeless people, then that would be a testament for supporting more need-specific services: e.g., more local control of benefits. Finally, it would be disingenuous not to admit that my aspiration to do follow-up research in an urban area is also deeply rooted in my desire to return to Camden, New Jersey, to collect the narratives of loved ones and friends, and to reconnect with the homeless population in a city where this research began over ten years ago. "Part I" of this book captured my experiences while living in Camden and it is important that those with whom these experiences were shared also have an opportunity to tell their stories.

10. Epilogue

When considering the interactions had during this research, I constantly return to a story written in 2008. The story focuses on the deep friendship I had developed with Akeem while living in Camden. After working with him at the homeless shelter, Frank's Place, for several months, I crossed paths with him near the Camden Waterfront on a weekend afternoon. We spoke briefly about work and about seeing each other on Monday morning. When we parted, we hugged each other and Akeem said, "I love you" (Phillips, 2008). Wrapped in these simple words were complex feelings of honesty, trust, compassion, and care. To this day, Akeem and I remain close. We speak on the phone about once a month and occasionally go out to eat. I send him postcards from my travels and he sends me pictures of his daughter. And even though Akeem's a Muslim, he's generous enough to humor me every year when we get together and exchange Christmas presents.

This story is shared as a reminder of why narrative-centered research is important. I have worked and volunteered with the homeless for more than a decade and have developed close relationships with many of the people with whom I have worked. As an academic, I am interested in asking critical questions and solving difficult problems. However, as a friend to many people who are homeless, I simply want policies to work so that my loved ones can successfully transition off the streets and into housing. Homelessness is a problem begging for well-reasoned academic solutions and for reasons already highlighted, I am not convinced that simply throwing money at failed policies is part of that solution. Instead, academics have to interact and talk with the homeless about their lives, their needs, and their long-term goals. The academy holds power and scholarly recommendations carry weight with the politicians who create policy. Therefore, embracing narrative-driven research and prioritizing dialogue between the homeless and

174

scholars is important. If scholars want to make recommendations about what the homeless need, then scholars need to develop relationships with the homeless. While this research is limited, it remains a hope that this research might persuade some readers to embrace more inclusive dialogue with the homeless because without considering their perspectives, all the money-driven policies in the world will not end homelessness.

Of course the narrative approach is not without its imperfections. For example, because narrative-driven research is located in the intimate experiences of the participants, there is a tendency to want to find closure for these personal stories. Readers want to know "the ending," and one emotionally-charged story can create academic tunnel-vision that begs for answers to questions such as, "Did Kenneth ever find work?" or "Did Philip and Ashley ever get their child back?" Unfortunately, the answer to both these questions is "I don't know." While these questions are significant, it is important to avoid academic tunnel-vision and to balance our desire for narrative closure with larger understandings about the cultural systems that drive homelessness. In short, narrative-driven scholars need quantitative research to help us put our work in perspective. The narratives of the homeless are daunting and can sometimes feel hopeless, but if scholars use these narratives as a way to craft better-functioning policies at a systemic level, then I am confident that we will witness progress.

At the same time, scholars who willingly share their expertise about the quantitative aspects of homelessness must also be willing to receive the embodied expertise of homeless people if an honest and productive intercultural dialogue about homelessness is ever to take place. Moving forward as a scholar engaged with homeless populations, I continually reflect on what research can mean when we choose to engage with people on such an intimate level as to gain their trust and their love. My year in Camden was rooted in trust and love, which allowed for the mutual exchange of personal respect, personal insights, and personal narratives. A decade later, the research in southern Illinois was performed in a similar spirit. In the end, I want to produce good research because I want homeless people to know (not just feel, but know) that they have a voice in public debates about food security, affordable housing, and other public benefits. I want homeless people to know that their voices matter. Additionally, I want to be a good academic writer so that these voices will be heard by non-homeless people who influence public policy and shelter policy. Through this and future research, scholars can continue creating spaces within the academy where homeless people share their narratives and where scholars embrace these narratives as critical sites of knowledge production. This is only one research project, but it is the first step toward creating this sort of academic inclusion. The second step involves sharing these findings with shelters, caseworkers, politicians, volunteers, and other community organizations committed to ending homelessness. In doing so, we can provoke critical dialogue that challenges policymakers to abandon failing social programs that currently ignore the voices of the homeless and instead consider how the voices of the homeless are essential in creating new and more effective policies.

Appendix A:
List of Participants
and Demographics

Pseudonym	Age	Gender	Race	Hometown/ Previous Residence	Duration of Homelessness*
Brandon	38	Male	White	Western KY	6 months
Philip**	49	Male	Black	Carbondale, IL	8 months
Ashley**	35	Female	White	Carbondale, IL	8 months
Kristen	42	Female	Biracial Black/White	Cape Girardeau, MO	2 months
James	61	Male	White	Southern IL	2 years (on and off)
Maddy	30	Female	Biracial White/Latina	Southern IN	1 month
Kenneth	46	Male	White	Carterville, IL	5 years
Tiffany	47	Female	White	Carbondale, IL	4 years (on and off)
Joe	34	Male	White	Carbondale, IL	1 year
Michael	37	Male	White	Herrin, IL	6 weeks

*All durations are continuous unless marked otherwise, and are dated as of August 15, 2013, the final date for data collection.

**Philip and Ashley were married to each other and were interviewed separately.

Appendix B:
Guiding Interview
Questions

1. Could you tell me a little bit about yourself? Name? Age? Where you are from?
2. How did you arrive at Good Samaritan Ministries?
3. Where were you before you arrived at Good Samaritan Ministries?
4. Tell me about some of your experiences.
    a. What are some of the challenges about being homeless?
    b. What are some of the biggest surprises?
5. Besides Good Sam's, where else have you gone for resources?
6. Could you tell me about some of the resources/services you receive?
    a. How do you use those services?
    b. Do you use those services for their intended purpose?
7. Have you received resources/services from both charitable and government agencies?
    a. What are some of the differences?
    b. Do you have a preference?
8. Tell me about a positive experience you had while being homeless.
    a. Is there a particular resource/service that helped you?
    b. Is there a particular person who helped you?
9. What resources do you feel are missing? (housing, food, jobs, etc.)
10. If you could create an organization that helped the homeless, what would that organization look like? What would it do? How would it help?
11. What do you want to tell service providers that could help them be more responsive and sensitive to your needs?

12. What piece of advice would you give to other homeless people who are new to the system? What will be their biggest challenge, in your opinion?

13. What do you want to tell people who are not homeless about being homeless?

14. Is there anything else you would like to share? Any other experiences or stories?

Bibliography

Anderberg, K. (2011). *21st Century Essays on Homelessness*. Ventura, CA: Seaward Avenue Press.

Becker, H. S. (1986). *Writing for Social Scientists*. Chicago, IL: University of Chicago Press.

Blackwell, K. (2012, September 04). Mr. Obama's America: "where everything's free but us." *Townhall*. Retrieved from http://townhall.com/columnists/kenblackwell/2012/09/04/ mr_obamas_america_where_everythings_free_but_us

Bloomberg bans food donations to NYC homeless shelters. (2012, March 20). *Huffington Post*. Retrieved from http://www.huffingtonpost.com/2012/03/20/bloomberg-bans-food-donat_n_1367542.html

Briquelet, K. (2013, January 7). Welfare recipients take out cash at strip clubs, liquor stores and x-rated shops. *New York Post*, Retrieved from http://www.nypost.com/p/news/local/ poor_some_sugar_on_me_0Hq1d3iPnvj2RwpsEDS7MN

Burke, K. (1968). Definition of man. In K. Burke (Ed.), *Language and Symbolic Action: Essays on Life, Literature, and Method*. (pp. 3–24). Berkeley: University of California Press.

Bute, J. J., & Jensen, R. E. (2011). Narrative sensemaking and time lapse: Interviews with low-income women about sex education. *Communication Monographs*, 78(2), 212–232.

Campbell, R., & Reeves, J. L. (1989). Covering the homeless: The Joyce Brown story. *Critical Studies in Mass Communication*, 6(1), 21–42.

Carspecken, P. F. (1996). *Critical Ethnography in Education Research: A Theoretical and Practical Guide*. New York: Routledge.

Cloke, P., Johnsen, S., & May, J. (2007). Ethical citizenship?: Volunteers and the ethics of providing services for homeless people. *Geoforum*, 38(6), 1089–1101.

Congressional Research Service. (2012, October 16). Memorandum: Spending for federal benefits and services for people with low income, FY2008-FY2011: An update of table B-1 from CRS report R41625, modified to remove programs for veterans. Retrieved from http://www.scribd.com/doc/110366590/Spending-for-Federal-Benefits-and-Services-for-People-With-Low-Income-FY08-FY11

Conover, T. (1984). *Rolling Nowhere: Riding the Rails with America's Hoboes*. New York: Vintage Departures.

Daniel, J. (1970). The poor: aliens in an affluent society: cross-cultural communication. *Communication Quarterly*, 18, 15–21.

Denzin, N. K. (1997). *Interpretive Ethnography: Ethnographic Practices for the 21st Century*. Thousand Oaks, CA: Sage.

DePastino, T. (2003). *Citizen Hobo: How a Century of Homelessness Shaped America*. Chicago, IL: The University of Chicago Press.

DeTurk, S. (2001). Intercultural empathy: Myth, competency, or possibility for alliance-building? *Communication Education*, 50(4), 374–385.

Disability insurance. (2014, January). *United States Department of Labor*, Retrieved from http://www.dol.gov/dol/topic/benefits-other/disabilityins.htm

Duneier, M. (2001). *Sidewalk*. New York: Farrar, Straus and Giroux.

Evans, M. A. W., ed. (1988). *Homeless in America*. Washington, D.C.: Acropolis Books.

Feldman, L. C. (2004). *Citizens Without Shelter. Homelessness, Democracy, and Political Exclusion*. Ithaca, NY: Cornell University Press.

Finley, S. (2010). Freedom's just another word for nothin' left to lose: The power of poetry for young, nomadic women of the streets. *Cultural Studies/Critical Methodologies, 10*(1), 58–63.

Fisher, W. R. (1987). *Human Communication as Narration: Toward a Philosophy of Reason, Value, and Action*. Columbia: University of South Carolina Press.

_____ (1984). Narration as a human communication paradigm: The case of public moral argument. *Communication Monographs, 51*(1), 1–22.

Flaccus, G. (2012, October 8). Cities impose new regulations on homeless amid tightening budgets. *Huffington Post*, Retrieved from http://www.huffingtonpost.com/2012/10/08/cities-homeless-regulations-budgets_n_1947719.html

Fussell, P. (1992). *Class: A Guide Through the American Status System*. New York: Touchstone.

Gibson, M. (2010, November 10). What's the most dangerous city in America? *Time Magazine*, Retrieved from http://newsfeed.time.com/2010/11/22/whats-the-most-dangerous-city-in-america/

Gillette, H. (2005). *Camden After the Fall: Decline and Renewal in a Post-Industrial City*. Philadelphia: University of Pennsylvania Press.

Ginsberg, H. (2012, October 18). Welfare spending up 32% in last 4 years. *Townhall*, Retrieved from http://townhall.com/tipsheet/heatherginsberg/2012/10/18/welfare_spending_up_32_ in_last_4_years

González, A. (2010). Reflecting upon "Enlarging Conceptual Boundaries: A Critique of Research in Intercultural Communication." In T.K. Nakayama and R.T. Halualani (Eds.), *The Handbook of Critical Intercultural Communication*. (pp. 53–56). Malden, MA: Wiley-Blackwell.

Gubruim, J. F., & Holstein, J. A. (2012) Narrative practice and the transformation of interview subjectivity. In J. F. Gubrium, J. A. Holstein, A. B. Marvasti, & K. D. McKinney (Eds.), *The SAGE Handbook of Interview Research: The Complexity of the Craft*. (2nd ed.). (pp. 27–43). Los Angeles: Sage.

Hall, W. (2012, October 15). Report: Illegal underground food stamp market thrives online. *Breitbart*, Retrieved from http://www.breitbart.com/Big-Government/2012/10/15/Report-Underground-Food-Stamp-Market-Thrives-Online

Halualani, R. T., & Nakayama, T. K. (2010). Critical intercultural communication studies: At a crossroads. In T. K. Nakayama and R. T. Halualani (Eds.), *The Handbook of Critical Intercultural Communication*. (pp. 1–16). Malden, MA: Wiley-Blackwell.

Hollis, M. (1977). *Models and Man: Philosophical Thoughts on Social Action*. Cambridge: Cambridge University Press.

Homeless camping ban: Denver city council passes city-wide "urban camping" ban. (2012, May 15). *Huffington Post*, Retrieved from http://www.huffingtonpost.com/2012/05/15/ homeless-camping-ban-denv_n_1517558.html

hooks, b. (2000). *Where We Stand: Class Matters*. New York: Routledge.

Huey, L., & Berndt, E. (2008). "You've gotta learn how to play the game": Homeless women's use of gender performance as a tool for preventing victimization. *Sociological Review, 56*(2), 177–194.

Iacono, J., Brown, A., & Holtham, C. (2009). Research methods: A case example of participant observation. *The Electronic Journal of Business Research Methods,* 7(1), 39–46.

Income security: Overlapping disability and unemployment benefits should be evaluated for potential savings. (2012, July 31). *U.S. Government Accountability Office,* Retrieved from http://www.gao.gov/products/D02946

Jamieson, D. (2012, September 05). Charlotte homeless outside DNC cling to motels. *Huffington Post,* Retrieved from http://www.huffingtonpost.com/2012/09/05/charlotte-homeless-dnc-motels_n_1856005.html

Katz, C. (2008, July 16). Take Denver homeless to the movies during Democratic National Convention! *New York Daily News,* Retrieved from http://articles.nydailynews.com/2008-07-16/news/17902216_1_denver-zoo-iacino-free-movie-tickets

Kozol, J. (2006). *Rachel and Her Children: Homeless Families in America.* New York: Random House.

Kulash, T. (2011, September 14). Midwest poverty rates rise to 13.9 percent. *The Daily Egyptian,* pp. 1, 3.

Lang, K. (2007). *Poverty and Discrimination.* Princeton, NJ: Princeton University Press.

Leeds-Hurwitz, W. (1990). Notes in the history of intercultural communication: The foreign service institute and the mandate for intercultural training. *Quarterly Journal of Speech,* 76(3), 261–281.

Lindemann, K. (2007). A tough sell: Stigma as souvenir in the contested performances of San Francisco's homeless street sheet. *Text & Performance Quarterly,* 27(1), 41–57.

Lundahl, B. W., & Wicks, L. (2010). The need to give and the need to receive: Volunteerism in homeless shelters. *Journal of Human Behavior in the Social Environment,* 20(2), 272–288.

MacDonald, H. (2000). *The Burden of Bad Ideas: How Modern Intellectuals Misshape Our Society.* Chicago, IL: Ivan R. Dee.

Mach, A. (2012, August 30). One of the most dangerous cities in the U.S. plans to ditch police force. *NBC News,* Retrieved from http://usnews.nbcnews.com/_news/2012/08/30/13504614-one-of-most-dangerous-cities-in-us-plans-to-ditch-police-force?lite

Martin, J. N., & Nakayama, T. K. (1999). Thinking dialectically about culture and communication. *Communication Theory,* 9(1), 1–25.

May, C. (2012, October 18). Report: Welfare government's single largest budget item in FY 2011 at approx. $1.03 trillion. *Daily Caller,* Retrieved from http://dailycaller.com/2012/10/18/report-welfare-governments-single-largest-budget-item-in-fy-2011-at-approx-1-03-trillion/

Mendoza, S. L. (2005). Bridging paradigms: How not to throw out the baby of collective representation with the functionalist bathwater in critical intercultural communication. *International and Intercultural Communication Annual,* 23, 237–256.

Mileur, E. (2011, November 7). Good Samaritans seek assistance in aiding poor. *The Daily Egyptian,* pp. 1, 3.

Miller, P., Donahue, P., Este, D., & Hofer, M. (2004). Experiences of being homeless or at risk of being homeless among Canadian youth. *Adolescence,* 39(156), 735–755.

Minnich, E. K. (1986). *Conceptual Errors Across the Curriculum: Towards a Transformation of the Tradition* (Memphis Research Clearinghouse and Curriculum Integration Project). Memphis, TN: Memphis State University, Center for Research on Women.

Montalbano-Phelps, L. L. (2004). *Taking Narrative Risk: The Empowerment of Abuse Survivors*. Dallas: University Press of America.

Moon, D. G. (1996). Concepts of "Culture": Implications for intercultural communication research. *Communication Quarterly, 44*(1), 70–84.

_____. (2010). Critical reflections on culture and critical intercultural communication. In T. K. Nakayama and R. T. Halualani (Eds.), *The Handbook of Critical Intercultural Communication*. (pp. 34–52). Malden, MA: Wiley-Blackwell.

Moss, K. (2003). *The Color of Class: Poor Whites and the Paradox of Privilege*. Philadelphia: University of Pennsylvania Press.

Murray, C. (2012). *Coming Apart: The State of White America, 1960–2010*. New York: Crown Forum.

_____. (1984). *Losing Ground: American Social Policy 1950–1980*. New York: Basic Books.

_____. (1992). Preface. In M. Olasky (Ed.), *The Tragedy of American Compassion* (pp. xi–xvii). Wheaton, IL: Crossway Books.

National Alliance to End Homelessness. (2011, January 11). State of homelessness in America 2012. Retrieved from http://www.endhomelessness.org/library/entry/the-state-of-homelessness-in-america-2012

National Coalition for the Homeless. (2009, July). How many people experience homelessness? Retrieved from http://www.nationalhomeless.org/factsheets/How_Many.html

National Law Center on Homelessness & Poverty. (2004, January). Increasing homelessness in the United States violates international law. Retrieved from http://www.nlchp.org/view_release.cfm?PRID=26

New census statistics paint grim picture of Camden. (2012, September 22). *Philadelphia Inquirer*, Retrieved from, http://www.philly.com/philly/blogs/camden_flow/170812236.html

Noah, T. (2012). *The Great Divergence: America's Growing Inequality Crisis and What We Can Do About It*. New York: Bloomsbury Press.

Norris, D. W. (2013, January 20). Hard times in the region: Six of state's nine most impoverished counties call Southern Illinois home. *The Southern Illinoisan*, pp. 1A, 5A.

Nouwen, H. J. M. (2004). *Out of Solitude: Three Meditations on the Christian Life*. Notre Dame, IN: Ave Maria Press.

Olasky, M. (1992). *The Tragedy of American Compassion*. Wheaton, IL: Crossway Books.

Pearce, M. (2012, June 11). Homeless feeding ban: Well-meaning policy or war on the poor? *Los Angeles Times*, Retrieved from http://articles.latimes.com/2012/jun/11/nation/la-na-nn-homeless-feeding-bans-20120611

Pelias, R. J. (2011). Writing into position: Strategies for composition and evaluation. In N. K. Denzin & Y. S. Lincoln (Eds.), *The SAGE Handbook of Qualitative Research*. (4th ed.). (pp. 659–668). Los Angeles: Sage.

Philipsen, G. (1976). Places for speaking in Teamsterville. *Quarterly Journal of Speech, 62*, 15–25.

Phillips, J. (2008). I love you. In L. Barber (Ed.), *New Neighbor: An Invitation to Join Beloved Community*. (p. 163). Atlanta: Mission Year.

Profits from poverty: How food stamps benefit corporations. (2012, September). *Government Accountability Institute*, Retrieved from http://g-a-i.org/wp-content/uploads/2012/10/GAI-Report-ProfitsfromPoverty-FINAL.pdf

Prois, J. (2012, August 13). Philadelphia homeless feeding ban officially blocked by judge. *Huffington Post*, Retrieved from http://www.huffingtonpost.com/2012/08/13/ philadelphia-homeless-feeding-ban_n_1773438.html

Ravenhill, M. (2008). *The Culture of Homelessness*. Burlington, VA: Ashgate.

Riis, J. A. (1890). *How the Other Half Lives: Studies Among the Tenements of New York*. New York: Charles Scribner's Sons.

Romeo, N. (2012, October 1). Camden, N.J. named poorest city in the United States, replacing Reading, Pa. *The Review*, Retrieved from http://www.udreview.com/camden-n-j-named-poorest-city-in-the-united-states-replaces-reading-pa-1.2916241#.UQR3wPIXA2Y

Rosen, M. (2007). The problem of homelessness is exaggerated. In L. Gerdes (Ed.), *The Homeless* (pp. 26–29). Detroit, MI: Thomson Gale.

Rossi, P. (1989). *Without Shelter: Homelessness in the 1980s*. New York: Priority.

Rowland, R. C. (1987). Narrative: Mode of discourse or paradigm? *Communication Monographs, 54*(3), 264–275.

Schiff, L. (1990). Would they be better off in a home? *National Review, 42*(4), 32–35.

Scott, J., & Leonhardt, D. (2005). Shadowy lines that still divide us. In Correspondents of *The New York Times* (Eds.), *Class Matters*. (pp. 1–26). New York: Times Books.

Senators introduce bipartisan legislation to reduce overlapping benefit payments. (2013, June 6). *Tom Coburn: Press Room*, Retrieved from http://www.coburn.senate.gov/public/index.cfm/pressreleases?ContentRecord_id=5f02f5ef-31f3-435e-a5ac-3a217dbedd87 &ContentType_id=d741b7a7-7863-4223-9904-8cb9378aa03a&Group_id=7a55cb96-4639-4dac-8c0c-99a4a227bd3a

Shipler, D. K. (2005). *The Working Poor: Invisible in America*. New York: Vintage.

Smiley, T., & West, C. (2012). *The Rich and the Rest of Us: A Poverty Manifesto*. New York: SmileyBooks.

Stier, J. (2012, March 18). No kugel for you! Mike's homeless-gift ban. *New York Post*, Retrieved from http://www.nypost.com/p/news/opinion/opedcolumnists/ no_kugel_for_you_N4VuTrqavfOiApSHngxuMJ

Tareen, S. (2011, September 18). Illinois poverty growing as state help shrinking. *The Southern Illinoisan*, p. 4B.

Terkel, S. (1993). *Division Street America*. New York: New Press.

_____. (1970). *Hard Times: An Oral History of the Great Depression*. New York: Pantheon Books.

Toulmin, S. E. (1970). Reasons and causes. In R. Borger & F. Cioffi (Eds.), *Explanations in the Behavioral Sciences*. (pp. 1–41). Cambridge: Cambridge University Press.

Unemployment insurance. (2014, January). *United States Department of Labor*, Retrieved from http://www.dol.gov/dol/topic/unemployment-insurance/

United States Census Bureau. (2010). Camden (city), New Jersey. Retrieved from, http://quickfacts.census.gov/qfd/states/34/3410000.html

Van De Mieroop, D. (2011). Identity negotiations in narrative accounts about poverty. *Discourse & Society, 22*(5), 565–591.

Volunteers of America Delaware Valley. (2010). *Volunteers of America Delaware Valley Annual Report*. Retrieved from, http://www.voadv.org/2010-Annual-Report

Walsh, M. E. (1992). *"Moving to Nowhere": Children's Stories of Homelessness*. New York: Auburn House.

Wasserman, J. A., & Clair, J. M. (2010). *At Home on the Street: People, Poverty & A Hidden Culture of Homelessness*. Boulder, CO: Lynne Rienner.

Whiting, G. C. (1971). Code restrictedness and opportunities for change in developing countries. *Journal of Communication, 21*, 36–57.

Williams, B. (2007). Life as narrative. *European Journal of Philosophy, 17*(2), 305–314.

Williams, J. C. (2003). *"A Roof Over My Head": Homeless Women and the Shelter Industry*. Boulder: University Press of Colorado.

Williams, W. E. (2011). *Race & Economics: How Much Can Be Blamed on Discrimination*. Stanford: Hoover Institute Press Publication.

Wilson, W. J. (1996). *When Work Disappears: The World of the New Urban Poor*. New York: Vintage.

Winkler, A., & Gillespie, N. (2012, November 21). Philadelphia: No love for the homeless: Charities continue suit against city's ban on feeding homeless outdoors. *Reason*, Retrieved from http://reason.com/reasontv/2012/11/21/philadelphia-no-love-for-the-homeless

Index

abuse: allegations 97; benefit 128, 131–32; charity 136–39; family 136, 137; monitoring 19–20; sexual 61–62; shelter 63, 139, 143; system 128, 139; 20/20 32; verbal 85; *see also* drugs

accountability: encouraged 166; individual and systemic 133; recipient 166; result of none 133, 135; shelter policy 167–68, 170

addict: attitude 20, 135; cause of homelessness 55; children 21; counseling 58; crack 20, 39, 67; employment 118; family 20; heroin 21, 90, 125; LaKeesha 21–22; marks 20, 24, 39; Martin 39–40; Marvin 20–21; meth 41; methadone 90; past 118; pregnant 21; rehab 167; self-described 20–21, 150; shelter 10, 24, 59, 110, 112, 167; stealing 27; struggle 151; support of 60, 68; term as cover for discrimination 110; *20/20* 31

agency 162; lack of 163

alcohol *see* drugs

Alcoholics Anonymous (AA) 151, 168

alliance 61, 74

Ashley (research participant): charity 123, 136; daughter 92, 96–97, 112, 123, 124, 137; demographics 177; father 137–38; Good Sam's 112–13; husband, Philip 154–55; money 136; Monty, Don 122–23; panhandling 85, 91–92, 122–23, 148, 154–55, 156; pride 99; propositioned 91–92; public aid 124, 135; swindled 86–87; The Women's Center 113; worry 100; *see also* Philip

attitude: anxiety 124; of the apathetic 46; cautious 16; desperation 153; guilt 62; about homeless 89; no

snitching 25; nonverbal cues 144; philosophical 15; pride 99, 120, 121; selling food stamps 142; shame 54, 62, 82, 88, 99, 116, 120; shelter employee's 46; state of mind 150; tentative 16; about violence 23; wary 16; *see also* reaction

banning 77, 84, 106, 107, 108

begging 40, 124; *see also* panhandling

behavior: "appropriate" 54; assumptions 159–60; choice 136; control of 53–54, 85, 113; employment 118; Good Sam's 83, 106, 140; illegal 132, 134, 162; irresponsible 103–4; monitored 53; public resources 84; shelter policy 167; subsidizing 69; tolerating 25; and work 37

belonging 144, 146, 157

benefit, government: concurrent 128–29; distribution 166; idea for improving 119; public policy 164; questions about 6, 75, 83; relinquishing 114; screening process 124; selling 67–68, 131, 134; time 116; useless 68; voice 69; volunteer work 119; work 166; *see also* abuse; disability insurance; food stamps/Link card; unemployment insurance

bilingual people 36; *see also* Spanish speaker

Bloomberg, Michael 57

Brandon (research participant): demographics 177; disability insurance 127–28; failure 120; family 95, 152; felony record 89–90, 121; food 130; food stamps 133–34; helping one another 156–57; job 89, 127, 152; prison 87–88, 110–11; roommates

187

Philip (research participant): appreciation for donations 123–24, 148–49; crying 101; demographics 177; employment 97, 98, 116–119; family 95, 97–98; helping others 156; media story 148–49; panhandling 85, 116–17, 119, 139, 154–55, 156; property 92–93; solution 119–20; suicidal thoughts 102; swindled 86–87; wife, Tiffany 154–55

phone: answering as job 28, 37; applying for benefits 124; lack of 28, 81; selling 132, 134–35, 136

police: asked for permission 107; fear of 26; monitoring drugs 19–20; no snitching culture and 26–27; and panhandling 122, 155; and public acts 84; questioning people 18; responsibility 88; stopping food-stamp sale 131

policy: better benefit 132; compassionate 163; Conservatives' 2; debate 171, 172; economic 1, 7, 47, 51, 57, 75; failed, throwing money at 47, 174; financial 47, 53; fostering positive results 163; health 53; housing 53, 57; implications for 164–67; influence on 176; intentions 163; Liberals' 2; money-driven 175; no-tolerance policy 19; policymakers 146; political 58, 160; poverty 57; shelter 167–68, 171; social 1, 7, 47, 51, 75; work requirement 166, 167; *see also* policy, public

policy, public: better-informed 66; crafting 68, 159; debating 71, 72, disciplining 57; implications 164; language in 56; points of concern 141–42; shaping 74; voices in 159, 164, 171, 176; work requirements 166

policymakers: abandoning failed programs 176; avoiding the homeless 53; listening 8, 143, 164–65; Philip's solution 119–20; questions to ask 145–46

politician 74, 145, 157, 159, 163, 172, 176

poverty: choice 54; end result 54–55; funding welfare programs 46; industry 46; laziness 55; making it out of 56, 89; as personal choice 55; race 55; rate 5, 46, 47, 76; realities 52, 68;

unchanged 7, 46, 47; work 89; *see also* Johnson, Lyndon B.

poverty tourism 30, 34

power 49, 50, 51, 53; imbalance of 161

prison 87, 88, 111, 112, 127

privacy 15, 35, 40, 107, 112; assistance guilt 62 lack of 62, 162; loss of 62–63, 82–85, 162; sex 83–84; social norms 162; on the streets 107; stress from losing 79

program: assistance 96, 131; drug treatment 39; failed government 46; lack of resources 124; most influence on homelessness 124; needs not met 133; no universal standards 58; political 8; social 176; social/social welfare 8, 139, 159; tracking 45; welfare 8, 46, 47, 48, 53, 74, 110

property 26, 61, 92–93, 146

prostitution 23–24, 39, 42, 112; *see also* sex

protection 11, 54, 61, 62, 63, 92, 132; *see also* safety

public feeding 57

race/racism 49, 55, 78; barrier to shelters 109–10; hoboes as 52; research participants' 177; *see also* student

rape *see* crime

reaction: to being homeless 99, 101; crying 92, 101–2; embarrassment 99, 100, 116, 120; pride 120, 121; suicide 101, 102; violent 100–101; worry 100; *see also* attitude

reality: addressing 68, 143; culture 49; cycle 42–43; daily 66; drugs and white America 18–19; employment 89; and food stamps, money 117, 129–30; lower-class 47; and macro system 49; of no privacy 62; oppressive 55; person's position 49, 52; reflecting 72; of scam 141; shaping 49; socially constructed 51; vulnerable 7, 78; *see also* struggle; support

record, criminal/felony 87, 88, 110, 135; effect of 89–90, 118, 125; policy against 122, 167; *see also* crime; felon

Reducing Overlapping Payment Act (2013) 129

relationship: abusive 61–62; accountability 133; community 153; criminal

volunteer 29, 31, 41; appreciation for
123; attitude 14, 35, 65; barriers 64;
cash benefit requirement 119; connection 33–34; ending homelessness
176; finding 169; Frank's 6; good in-
tentions/will 30–31, 65, 145; hierarchy 35; influence 176; listening 74;
sacrifices 123; serving meals 57;
stipend 3, 38; student 20–21, 33
voucher 59, 67

wait: disability insurance 128, 135;
Frank's 42; job 152; 30 day limit 109;
wait list 126; winter 36
Walter Rand Transportation Center 9,
10, 12, 22, 27; eviction from 14;
Genevieve 13–14; as home 13–14;
Mr. Lawrence 15; personal relationships 35; safety 14, 21; sleeping at 5,
11, 15

War on Poverty 7, 47, 63
warrant: catch-and-release cycle 29;
exception to open door policy 167;
and Good Sam's 76, 83, 110; police
sweep 19; from two states 95; under
the radar from 135
water 61, 91, 108, 124
weapons 106; chain 23; Good Sam's
policy 106; penknife 27; pocketknife
19
weather: challenge 108; clothing 23–
24, 123; and disappearance 27; escaping 36; favorable 171; freezing 14,
147; during interviews 81; and job
28, 36; summer 40, 87, 107–8, 171;
and transportation center 15; winter
15, 21, 36, 140–41, 171
welfare programs *see* program: welfare
The Women's Center 113